Smoky Mountain
Hiking & Camping

Smoky Mountain Hiking & Camping

A Guide to the Great Smoky Mountains National Park

Lee Barnes

Menasha Ridge Press
Birmingham, Alabama

Library of Congress Cataloging-in-Publication Data
Barnes, Lee. 1954-
    Smoky Mountain hiking & camping: a guide to the Great Smoky Mountains National Park/Lee Barnes.
      p. cm.
    Includes bibliographical references and index.
    1. Hiking—Great Smoky Mountains National Park (N.C. and Tenn.)—Guidebooks. 2. Backpacking—Great Smoky Mountains National Park (N.C. and Tenn.)—Guidebooks. 3. Camp sites, facilities, etc.—Great Smoky Mountains National Park (N.C. and Tenn.) 4. Trails—Great Smoky Mountains National Park (N.C. and Tenn.)—Guidebooks. 5.Great Smoky Mountains National Park (N.C. and Tenn.)—Guidebooks.
I. Title II. Title: Smoky Mountain hiking & camping
GV199.42.G73B37   1994
796.5'1'0976889—dc20   94-37978
                                                          CIP

ISBN 0-89732-126-X

Book design by Frank Logue
Carolina Graphics Group, Inc.
Map design by Sue Irwin

Menasha Ridge Press
700 South 28th Street, Suite 206
Birmingham, Alabama 35233
1-800-247-9437
website at http://www.menasharidge.com

This labor of love is dedicated to Shorty and Alyse,
who carried me to trailheads during the early years
and who finally decided that I would be all right there
or at least I always made it home to resupply.

Table of Contents

Major rainstorms in late March 1994 resulted in extensive damage to Tennessee roads within the Park. Many footbridges along the lower ends of Tennessee trails also suffered damage. Roads listed as "indefinately closed" include Parsons Branch Road (connecting Cades Cove and Calderwood Lake), and the upper ends of Greenbrier Road and Tremont Road above Tremont Institute. Check with Park Information or Rangers for current status of roads.

1
Introduction

The Great Smoky Mountains National Park is our most popular national park, with approximately ten million visitors per year. It is also the largest national park east of the Mississippi. The locals refer to the Park as the "Smokies."

The Smokies, an estimated 517,000 acres of forest, contain the largest undeveloped forest in the southern Appalachians, an estimated 90% of the remaining virgin forest in the East. Large sections of forest along the higher ridges have never been logged except for selective cuttings of the highly-valued cherry and walnut trees.

The Smokies is the most botanically rich area in the country, containing over 120 different species of trees, approximately 1,800 species of plants, and nearly 2,000 species of mushrooms. With 26 species of salamanders, the Smokies is home to more species of salamanders than anywhere else in the world.

The Park roads and trails allow easy access to the most spectacular scenery in the East. The Smokies contain the most extensive maintained trail system in the country, with over 900 miles of trail for hikers and horseback riders.

The Park can be roughly visualized as a 55-mile long by 20-mile wide, oval shaped preserve that is orientated east-west along the central section of the border of North Carolina and Tennessee. The Park contains the largest mass of mountains in the East, with more mountain peaks above 5,000 and 6,000 thousand feet than anywhere else along the entire Appalachian Mountain Range. The Smokies are officially designated as an International Biotic Reserve, with on-going legislation and management to designate most of the Park as a Federal Wilderness Area.

The geology of the Smokies is very complex. The mountains are composed mostly of heavily-eroded sedimentary rocks fractured by numerous fault-zones and geological "non-conformities." The present mountains are the mere roots of an ancient, colossal mountain range, which is believed to have been as high as (or higher than) the present Himalayas. King et al (1968) and Moore (1988) provide an excellent summary of the area's geological history and present conditions (see Appendix A).

The Park is dominated by the main "backbone" ridge, which extends 50 miles in length "as the crow flies," running from south-west to northeast. The Appalachian Trail (A.T.) follows primarily along the highest part of the ridge, which also is the North Carolina and Tennessee border. Major lateral ridges form "skeletal ribs" and are separated by deep valley stream drainages.

One such rib, the Balsam Mountain Range, intercepts the main Smokies ridge along its eastern third and connects east-west with the geologically distinct Blue Ridge Mountain Range. The southern end of the Blue Ridge Parkway follows along the crest of the Balsam Mountain Range from Richland Balsam Mountain to Big Witch Gap, and descends to the Park entrance near the town of Cherokee.

Only one road crosses the main ridge, the Newfound Gap Road, crossing at Newfound Gap (elevation 5,000 feet). This road effectively divides the Park into its western and eastern halves. From Newfound Gap, a seven-mile spur road, the Clingmans Dome Road, leads to Clingmans Dome (elevation 6,664 feet).

Clingmans Dome is the highest peak in the Smokies and the second highest in the East. East from Clingmans Dome, the ridge trail (the A.T.) travels through evergreen spruce and fir forest for 30 miles, where the trees and plants are similar to much more northern, Canadian-like forests.

The average height of the western half of the main ridge is 4,000 to 5,000 feet above the lowland valleys, which "bottom-out" at 1,500 to 2,000 feet in elevation. The western half of the main ridge is primarily covered by a deciduous, oak-hickory forest. The moist cove forests found below the ridge contain some of the most diverse plant life in North America. These mid-elevation cove forests are most spectacular in late April and early May when the forest floor is carpeted with a rich diversity of blooming wildflowers. Winter views are greatest from along the main ridge and major side ridges.

Along the eastern half of the Smokies, the main ridge averages 5,500 to 6,000 feet in elevation, an average of 3,500 to 5,000 feet above the surrounding valleys. Through this section of the Park, the famous A.T. follows the relatively narrow main ridge with few major elevation changes from Clingmans Dome to Mt. Cammerer, and then steeply descends to the eastern border of the Park at Davenport Gap, near I-40.

Large sections of the lower mountain slopes and valleys were heavily logged in the early 1920s and '30s, but these areas have regrown into impressive forests in the last 60 years. In general, the forests on the Tennessee side receive the more consistent rainfall than North Carolina and therefore have more large hemlocks. All of the higher elevations are temperate rain-forests and often receive over 90 inches of rain per year. A well-developed shrub understory is prevalent throughout the Park, making cross-country travel extremely slow, exhausting, and nearly impossible.

The extreme northwestern corner of the Park from Abrams Creek to Cades Cove is distinct from the rest of the Park. Here, the bedrock is geologically different with several broad, nearly level valleys and limestone sinkholes and "solution" caves. The forests along the low ridges on the Tennessee side have a higher percentage of pines and drought-tolerant oaks than in the rest of the Park.

The forest vegetation in the Park can be divided into eight major forest types: spruce-fir forests, heath balds, grassy balds, northern hardwood forests, hemlock forests, open oak-pine forests, closed oak forests and cove hardwood forests. Forest composition is strongly influenced by elevation, slope, and aspect/angle to the sun.

The most characteristic spruce-fir forest is found along the A.T.

from the western slopes of Clingmans Dome east 35 miles to Mt. Guyot generally shading the slopes above 5,000 and 6,000 feet. In these forests, the vegetation is often shrouded in clouds and fog, the trails are moist underfoot, and the air temperature is almost always cool.

It should be sadly noted that in these northern-type forests, the older, mature Fraser fir trees are dying, and the mature spruce trees have shown a sizeable decrease in growth rates and general vigor during recent years. This forest decline is presumably due to a combination of factors including insect attack, acid-fog and acid-rain, and suspected ozone pollution.

The weakened Fraser firs are also being attacked by a small aphid-like bug, the Wooly Balsam Adelgid. In some areas, over 90% of the fir trees are dead or declining, noticeable by increased brightness of the forest floor. It is expected that within a few more years, these beautiful evergreen forests will be replaced by a totally different type of tree and shrub cover, the populations of ferns and mosses will be reduced, and a major change will occur in the variety of small mammals, birds, and amphibians surviving there. Vast areas of fir seedlings can be seen along the higher elevations, but there is uncertainty about whether these seedlings will ever reach maturity and re-seed these mountain slopes.

Grassy Balds (Gregory Bald, Spence Field, Andrews Bald, etc.) are generally found along the western ridge at elevations near or above 5,000. These meadow-like areas present fantastic views and are noted for spectacular displays of flame azaleas.

Heath Balds (Maddon Bald, Brushy Mountain, etc.) consist of dense, impenetrable masses of rhododendron and mountain laurel with few or no trees. Locally, these are known as "slicks" because they appear to be smooth and solid when viewed from a distance. The purple rhododendron, or Catawba rhododendron, are especially beautiful along the higher elevations in May and early June.

Along a fairly narrow vegetation band at about 4,500 feet, there are the northern hardwood forests, comprised primarily of birch, beech, maple, cherry, scattered hemlock, and an occasional spruce tree. Often the high gaps and moist slopes are covered by sedge-grass and the general appearance is of maintained parkland.

The hemlock forests are found below 4,500 feet, with extensive stands along the wetter and northern slopes of the Park. In most of the Park, the hemlocks are usually restricted to stream banks and wet ravines, especially on the southern slopes. Other moisture-loving plants are found here such as maple, birch, beech, and tulip popular. Shrub "understories" include massive tangles of evergreen rhododendron and dog-hobble.

Along the middle and lower slopes below 4,000 feet, there are open oak-pine forests and the closed oak forests. The open oak-pine forests are found on the drier, more exposed southern and western slopes. These forests contain four to five different species of oak and pine, often with dense patches of evergreen rhododendron and laurel. The closed oak forests are found at low or middle elevations and contain hickory, maple, sourwood, tulip popular, black locust, dogwood, four species of oak, and various other shrubs. These areas are especially colorful during the fall.

The last forest type found in the Park is the cove hardwood forests, which occur in valleys and coves between 1,100 and 4,000 feet and contain the greatest variety of trees and wildflowers. These forests are dominated by sugar maples, birch, beech, cucumber magnolia, hemlock, cherry, basswood, and scattered rhododendrons. I find the cove forests most beautiful between April and early May when carpeted with spring wildflowers.

For more information about the vegetation, refer to the books by Stupka and Campbell (see Appendix B). The relatively inexpensive wildflower book by Campbell et al. contains numerous color photographs and additional plant descriptions.

The Roads

There are 270 miles of roads within the Park and two major and several minor, scenic roads that encircle the Park. Because travel through the mountains can be deceptive when looking at regional road maps, the following road descriptions are provided. They will help you choose between enjoyable and scenic routes or more rapid access between different Park sections.

Free maps and brochures describing the Park roads can be

obtained by writing or calling the Park Superintendent (see Appendix C). A 96-page, official guide to these roads, *Mountain Roads and Quiet Places*, is available from the visitor centers or from the Great Smoky Mountain Natural History Association (GSMNHA). This guide describes the roads through the Park and contains a key to the numbered roadside guideposts. The Knoxville Garden Club recently published a book, *Scenic Drives and Wildflower Walks in the Great Smokies*, which will give you more detailed information about scenic drives and trails that are well-known for wildflower viewing. The geology along the major roadsides is covered in the book by Harry Moore (see Appendix B).

Due to the nature of these winding mountain roads and traffic, plan travel times of at least twice as long as "flat-land" travel. You will generally average about 25 to 30 miles per hour. *Note:* There are no sources of gasoline within the Park and the cost of gasoline is generally much greater in the Park border towns like Gatlinburg and Cherokee. Try filling your tank 25 miles outside the Park.

In general, traffic flows well through the Park, but at a more "casual" pace. Most "car-tourist" areas are concentrated along three roads. The first is the Newfound Gap Road, or US 441 (closed to commercial traffic), which is the only road that crosses the main ridge. It connects the tourist towns of Cherokee and Gatlinburg and bumper-to-bumper traffic is common during "leaf-looker" season—early to mid-October.

The other two major roads are Clingmans Dome Road (a side road from Newfound Gap to the highest peak in the Park) and the roads from Gatlinburg to Cades Cove (Little River Road, Laurel Creek Road, and Cades Cove Road). Traffic movement may be extremely slow along these roads, so relax and enjoy the scenery!

Five roads are closed to RV's and cars pulling travel trailers because they are too narrow: Rich Mountain Road (gravel), Parson Cove Road (gravel), Roaring Fork Motor-way, Greenbrier Road (gravel), and Heintooga-Round Bottom Road (gravel). With the exception of Greenbrier Road, these roads are closed in the winter, usually from early November to the middle of April. Big Creek-Cataloochee Road (gravel), which follows the eastern border of the Park, is not recommended for RV's and trailers because it is narrow and winding.

Beginning along the extreme northeastern end of the Park, there is I-40, which travels through the spectacular Pigeon River Gorge into Tennessee. The North Carolina Welcome Center is seven miles from the state line and you can pick up a beautiful, free state map here. Unfortunately, this visitor center is only easily accessible from the east-bound lanes of I-40 as you enter from Tennessee.

There is a new (1993) Tennessee Welcome Center on I-40 between Waterville and the Foothills Parkway Exit. Shortly after entering Tennessee along I-40, the Foothills Parkway leads over low ridges, for 5.5 miles, with a spectacular view of the northeastern half of the Smokies. This section of the Foothills Parkway joins US 321 (TN 73) at a very widely dispersed community called Cosby. From here, it is only a short distance along TN 32 to the beautiful and seldom-full Cosby Campground.

TN 73 parallels the entire northern edge of the Park, connecting with the other completed section of the Foothills Parkway, an impressive 11-mile section around the western end of the Park. There are long term plans to complete the Foothills Parkway to parallel the entire northern border of the Park, but completion of this route has been delayed by environmental concerns and money restrictions.

TN 73 is labelled as Little River Road between Gatlinburg and Townsend. This road must be traveled slowly, but it is an extremely beautiful drive that is entirely within Park boundaries and passes through deep forests next to the Little River.

This scenic route connects with Laurel Creek Road, which leads to Cades Cove Campground and Cades Cove Loop Road. Cades Cove Loop Road encircles the scenic and historic Cades Cove Valley. TN 73 exits from the Park a few miles east of Cades Cove and travels into and through the community of Townsend and its famous Tuckaleechee Caves. From the Loop Road, Rich Mountain Road (a one-way gravel road that is closed in winter) exits north to Townsend and reconnects with TN 73. You may also leave Cades Cove via the seasonally open Parsons Branch Road (gravel), but this route bypasses the views from Chilhowee Mountain. A few miles west of Tuckaleechee Cove, TN 73 joins the 17-mile western section of the Foothills Parkway, which follows southward along Chilhowee Mountain.

There are impressive views all along this section of the Foothills Parkway east across the western end of the Park. The two sections of the Foothills Parkway are similar to the southern end of the Blue Ridge Parkway, but the Foothills Parkway offers more spectacular, close-up views of the Smokies. The Foothills Parkway ends at Calderwood Lake, where it joins US 129, a very curvy road around the western end of the Park that leads into North Carolina and joins NC 28 near Fontana Dam.

There is no road access to the southwestern third of the Park's southern border due to the filling of Fontana Lake in the mid-1940s. NC 28 generally runs close to the Smokies, allowing access to several national forest recreation sites, campgrounds and marinas along Fontana Lake. Near Bryson City, North Carolina, NC 28 joins US 19, the major road east along the rest of the southern border of the Park that leads through the town of Cherokee and crosses the Blue Ridge Parkway near Maggie Valley. The Blue Ridge Parkway leads southwest from Soco Gap and terminates at the Newfound Gap Road near the Oconaluftee Visitor Center, just north of Cherokee, North Carolina.

Another major highway, the Smoky Mountain Expressway (US 74/23) is four-lane between Bryson City and Waynesville with connections to US 276 and I-40. This road is removed from the Park borders, but it allows considerably more rapid travel along the southern edge of the Park and points east- and westward.

US 19 leads east through the heavily congested, tourist town of Maggie Valley to connect with US 276, which then leads northward through Jonathan Creek. This section of US 276 is a lightly traveled four-lane road, connecting with I-40 along the eastern edge of the Park. Immediately prior to the intersection of I-40 and NC 276, you will find Cove Creek Road. Cove Creek Road connects with Big Creek-Cataloochee Road (a gravel forest service road) that basically parallels I-40 above the Pigeon River Gorge.

This road connects with sections of paved roads north of Big Creek Ranger Station and beyond to Cosby, Tennessee. This is a much slower route (allow at least one hour to Cosby!) than I-40, but it is a more beautiful way to travel along the short, eastern edge of the Smokies. This route is not recommended for RV's or towed vehicles.

Big Creek-Cataloochee Road offers easy access to Park trails in Cataloochee Valley and the base of Mt. Sterling, the primitive Big Creek Campground, the trail to Walnut Bottoms, and the A.T.

Area Towns

Gatlinburg, Tennessee, and Cherokee, North Carolina, are the two largest area towns. They are located immediately outside the Park on US 441 at the northern and southern entrances, respectively. Both towns offer extensive tourist facilities (motels, campgrounds, convenience stores, tourist-traps, etc.).

Other nearby towns include Cosby, Pigeon Forge, and Townsend in Tennessee; and Fontana Village, Bryson City, Maggie Valley, and Waynesville in North Carolina. These towns offer private campgrounds, numerous groceries, camp supplies, shopping, and dining opportunities. (See Appendix C for Chamber of Commerce addresses.)

Gatlinburg is a major tourist center where 40% of the visitors enter the Park. Gatlinburg is humorously described as a "little Niagara Falls," with ski resorts, tee-shirt shops, incredible crowds in the summer, Ripley's Believe It or Not Museum Wax Museums, etc. Gatlinburg can accommodate over 33,000 overnight guests in its hotels and campgrounds. There is a low-cost ("trolley-car") shuttle bus system in Gatlinburg that greatly eases city travel and severe parking problems.

Cherokee, in many ways, is a scaled-down version of Gatlinburg. It can accommodate 3,200 overnight guests. In Cherokee, you will find an excellent Indian Museum and Craft Center, an authentic reconstruction of the Oconaluftee Indian Village (open from mid-May to October), and the award-winning outdoor theater, *Unto these Hills* (shows nightly from mid-June to late August). Unfortunately there are also numerous tourist-traps, souvenir shops, and legalized gambling ("Cherokee Bingo"). There are no major grocery stores in Cherokee—although light picnic foods are generally available. The Cherokee Travel and Tribal Promotion can provide an excellent guide to area events and lodging (see Appendix C).

Many western North Carolina towns and counties have unusual

liquor sales regulations. Some areas are completely "dry"—there are no sales of alcoholic beverages. Other areas allow beer sales but not wine, or wine but not beer, etc. The towns of Cherokee and Franklin are completely "dry." There are Alcoholic Beverage Control (ABC) stores in Bryson City, Maggie Valley, and Waynesville. (You may want to B.Y.O.B.)

Cosby is a small community located near I-40 at the northeastern end of the Park with limited groceries available along US 321. Cosby has a wonderful, regionally-acclaimed Mexican restaurant, The Front Porch, but it is only open on weekends (live local music on most Friday and Saturday nights). North of Gatlinburg on US 441, you will find the sprawling community of Pigeon Forge, which is a major resort and shopping area, known for its factory outlets, traffic, motels, and the Dollywood Resort Park. Townsend is a small community stretching for several miles along the northwestern end of the Park. It has limited groceries and camping supplies. There are numerous motels and campgrounds in the area.

Fontana Village, at the southwestern end of the Park, is a resort village with only limited groceries. Bryson City is on the southern border of the Park and contains several well-stocked grocery stores, including Ingles. The Great Smoky Mountain Railroad has a major station in Bryson City that is surrounded by small shops catering to tourists. Maggie Valley is another resort town next to the Park that only has small grocery stores. Waynesville, about six miles away, has a number of national chains including Bi-Lo, Winn-Dixie, Ingles, Wal-Mart, and K-Mart.

Visitor Centers

The two main visitor centers are located on the Newfound Gap Road at the entrances to the Park, near Gatlinburg and Cherokee. They are open from 8:00 A.M. to 6:00 P.M. (shorter hours in winter), seven days a week. Be sure to pick up a free copy of the award-winning *Smokies Guide*, the official Park newspaper that is produced four times a year. The *Smokies Guide* highlights seasonal attractions and lists current Park hours and regulations.

Sugarlands Visitor Center is located just inside the Park entrance near Gatlinburg, and is the largest visitor center in the Park. The displays are elaborate and there is an excellent bookstore, and a beautiful, introductory movie to the seasons and attractions of the Park. Expect to find crowds here! In the new addition to this visitor center, there is a separate backcountry office where trail information and permits can be obtained. You will still have to confirm your backcountry reservations or permit by telephone if your trip contains any rationed sites.

Oconaluftee Visitor Center is at the Park entrance near Cherokee. There are a few exhibits and a small gift and bookstore. There is also a self-service, backpacking registration center here. (If your trip involves use of any of the rationed campsites or shelters, you will have to call long-distance to the park headquarters near Gatlinburg to complete your registration.) At the Oconaluftee Visitor Center, there is a reconstructed pioneer homestead; and a few miles away you will find Mingus Mill, an operating "under-shot" grain mill and picnic grounds. There are plans to build a more complete, full-fledged visitor center at Oconoluftee, but funding for its construction is presently in limbo.

In addition to the main visitor centers, the Cades Cove Visitor Center is located half-way around Cades Cove Loop Road, just beyond the parking area for Abrams Falls. *Note:* This road is one-way and that prevents easy return from the visitor center to the trailhead for Abrams Falls. The Cades Cove Visitor Center is only open from mid-May to October. There is a nice museum that features photos and exhibits of the early pioneers; there are also some books for sale. Nearby you will find restored buildings and an old water mill.

Campgrounds

There are six developed car-camping campgrounds, three primitive campgrounds, and five auto-access horse camps in the Park. None of these campgrounds have electrical hook-ups or hot showers. The length of stay at developed and primitive campgrounds is limited to 7 consecutive days from May 15th through Labor Day and 14 consecutive days from Labor day to May 15th. Auto-access horse camps may be used for a maximum of 7 consecutive days. In late

Developed Campgrounds

Campground	Season	Sites	Elevation	Location
Balsam Mt.	Mid-May to mid-October	46	5310	10 miles N. of Soco Gap, off Blue Ridge Pkwy
Cades Cove	All year	161	1807	10 miles S.W. of Townsend, TN
Cosby	Mid-April to October	175	2459	20 miles E. of Gatlinburg, TN
Deep Creek	Early June	108	1800	2 miles N. of Bryson City, NC
Elkmont	All year	220	2150	9 miles W. of Gatlinburg, off TN 73
Look Rock	Late May to October	92	2600	11 miles N.W. from Wallard, TN on Foothills Pkwy
Smokemont	All year	140	2198	7 miles N. of Cherokee, NC on Newfound Gap Rd

1993, the number of available sites and the length of the operating season were reduced due to budget restrictions.

Three park campgrounds remain open year-round (Cades Cove, Elkmont, Cades Cove) and require phone reservations for sites between May 15th and October 30th. These campgrounds operate on a first-come, first-served basis from November through May 15th. All other car campgrounds operate on a first-come, first-served basis when seasonally open. To make campground phone reserva-

Primitive Campgrounds

Campground	Season	Sites	Elevation	Location
Abrams Creek	May to October	16	1125	At Abrams Ranger Station, extreme W. end of Park off the Foothills Parkway
Big Creek	Mid-April to October	12	1700	At Big Creek Ranger Station, E. end of Park near I-40
Cataloochee	Mid-April to October	27	2610	At Cataloochee Ranger Station, near I-40

tions, call 1-800-365-CAMP. Touch-tone phones are preferred or you can hold for a voice operator. You will need a credit card number and should be prepared to answer a series of questions including: which Park (Smokies Park code is GREA); which campground (Cades Cove, Elkmont, Smokemont); what dates; how many nights; how many campers (maximum six persons per site); what equipment you will be bringing (tent, RV, RV length); any pets; and any available discounts? Site availability will be confirmed immediately and reservations are completed with a credit card transaction.

The other car campsites in the Park are available on a first-come basis and are generally closed from November to mid-April. Cosby Campground, a beautiful, fully-developed campground, is located on the northeastern edge of the Park. It is less likely to be filled because it is located off of the main tourist routes. My favorite car campsites are Balsam Mountain (off the Blue Ridge Parkway between Maggie Valley and Cherokee) and Abrams Creek Campground (along the western end of the Park near Chilhowee Lake). These smaller, more out-of-the-way campgrounds may be filled on holidays or weekends, but they have an unique charm that is not obtainable at the larger campgrounds.

Automobile-access Horse Camps

Horse Camp	No. Horses	Location
Anthony Creek	12	Near Cades Cove Campground
Big Creek	20	Near I-40, Waterville Exit
Cataloochee	28	At the end of Cataloochee Rd.
Round Bottom	20	N.E. of Qualla Indian Reservation
Towstring	20	Near Smokemont Campground

Two of the primitive campgrounds, Big Creek Campground and Cataloochee Campground, are located along the eastern edge of the Park near I-40. Big Creek Campground has a new group campsite with new toilet buildings and enlarged horse camp facilities. The entire Cataloochee Watershed is a lot less crowded than other sections of the Park. The winding, gravel access roads are much less "inviting" to large vehicles or trailers. Look Rock Campground, listed on maps along the western Foothills Parkway, was closed for several years due to water problems, but was reopened in 1989.

The five auto-access horse camps in the Park are primitive campsites, designated specifically for campers with horses. They may be reserved up to 30 days in advance. At these horse camps, there is room for trucks and horse trailers, and you will also find primitive horse stalls. Unreserved sites are available on a first-come basis.

Outside the Park, there are numerous commercial campgrounds, but these are also heavily used. You can get a full listing of current private campgrounds from any local Chamber of Commerce (see Appendix C).

2
Hiking and Backpacking

Seasons and Weather

The Park is scenic and accessible year-round, but most people hike and camp from early May through late October. My favorite times in the Park are early spring when the cove wildflowers peak, mid-October when the leaves change colors, and early winter when the days are clear and sunny, and the bugs and tourists have been "thinned" by the first frost. The number of trail-users peaks from June to mid-August, remains high through mid-October, and then declines steeply in the winter.

The Smokies get a lot of rain, averages are between 50 and 90 inches per year. (Areas above 6,000 feet routinely receive over 90 inches!) The weather is often locally generated. Morning fogs evaporate and billow up the mountain slopes, only later to condense and form violent afternoon thunder showers. Daily afternoon showers are extremely common in the summer. (Be sure to always carry raingear!) The least rainfall is generally during September and October.

Air temperatures drop an average of 2.6° to 5° F for each 1,000 feet of elevation gained. I vividly remember 19° F and 25 mph winds on Balsam Mountain on the first of November that produced a wind chill equivalent of -10° F. There is a good chance of overnight freezing temperatures from September to mid-May. (Consider elevation and carry appropriate gear. Always be prepared for temperatures 10 to 15 degrees below the expected average.)

Daily weather reports can be obtained from visitor centers and from any of the radio-equipped rangers. Radio broadcasts by the National Oceanic and Atmosphere Administration (NOAA) can be received on the FM band at 162.475 out of Knoxville. Special weather radios can be obtained from electronics dealers such as Radio Shack.

Generally, I have been able to received NOAA weather reports whenever I was on a ridge, but reception is weak or impossible from the deep valleys. At times I have received weather reports from Chattanooga, Asheville, Knoxville, and Greenville (South Carolina). I find that the reports from Knoxville are usually the best for predicting upcoming weather changes in the Park because it is about a "weather-hour" away.

The table of average monthly temperatures in Gatlinburg gives an overview of the weather. These figures are based on the average for the last 37 years. Remember that air temperatures decrease an average of 2.6° to 5° F for each 1,000 feet in elevation gained. Western ridges average around 4,000 feet, and central and eastern ridges range between 5,000 and 6,000 feet. Northern lowlands are about 1,400 feet, southern lowlands are about 1700 feet, and Gatlinburg is about 1,200 feet.

Average Highs/Lows for Gatlinburg:
(*Note:* Record lows are shown in parentheses.)

January-	48/25 (-10)
February-	52/26 (-13)
March-	61/33 (-6)
April-	71/41 (19)
May-	78/49 (29)
June-	83/57 (33)
July-	86/61 (43)
August-	85/54 (32)
September-	81/54 (32)
October-	71/42 (15)
November-	60/32 (-3)
December-	52/27 (-12)

Clothing

Because of the likelihood of rain, be sure to carry a waterproof rain suit. Clothing (especially cotton fabrics) will not dry overnight because of the high humidity in the Smokies. I carry a complete change of dry clothes to wear in camp and change back into my damp day gear in the morning before hitting the trail in order to keep one set of dry clothes. Use any brief period of direct sun to dry equipment and clothing.

Because of the weather changes, be aware of the constant threat of hypothermia, the excessive loss of body heat caused by low temperatures and aggravated by windy conditions. It is best to dress in layers and always carry extra gear that is suitable for layering such as a pile pullover and outer windshell. Add a layer when you stop to rest and learn about the early signs of hyperthermia, which include difficulty in focusing and thinking, and mild to severe shivering.

Avoid cotton clothing because it offers little heat retention when wet and is very difficult to dry. Instead, use layers of wool or synthetic fibers such as polypropylene, which dries quickly and is warm even when wet.

Animals

Generally, the most bothersome animals found in the Park are the small mice that occupy all of the shelters. These mice will eat holes through your pack if they smell food inside. Chipmunks can also be a problem. They will boldly sneak into open food containers that are sitting at your feet. Skunks are generally only a problem in areas where the trash is not picked up.

In general, keep all food stored when not being prepared or consumed. You should plan to hang all food with "dead-man" guards (shields cut from plastic coffee can lids or jar tops with a hole punched in the center for the pack cord).

Small insects can be controlled with insecticides, especially products containing the highly effective repellent DEET. Mosquitos and gnats are seldom a problem on the trail, but biting deerflies have sometimes bothered me for miles. My most successful defense is to stop hiking, let the bugs land, and then quickly "squash `em." They are tough, so you may need to slap, roll, and then stomp them again!

While ticks are of little concern in the higher elevations, be aware of their presence. The main threat from ticks is the diseases they may carry. Rocky Mountain Tick Disease is more common in the piedmont areas of the southeast. Lyme Disease is carried by the small deer tick, which prefers deer or mice.

Lyme Disease is characterized by a serious skin rash, which expands in concentric circular patterns from the point of infection. This disease also produces flu-like symptoms that usually appear several days or weeks following infection. It is a good idea to note the date if you have to remove an attached tick. If these symptoms are observed, you should seek immediate medical help.

A general insecticide spray on your pant legs and tops of shoes and socks will repel most ticks. Ticks generally must be attached for several hours before they will transmit disease, so check your body several times during the day.

Secondary infections from improper tick removal are far more likely than these other diseases. Ticks may be difficult to remove once attached, so early detection and removal is important. Consult a recent outdoor medical book for recommended removal techniques. Be sure to thoroughly remove all mouth parts from the skin and treat the area with a general antibiotic cream.

Snakes and other "critters" will usually do their best to get out of your way before you see them. Of the 23 species of snakes reported in the Park, only two are poisonous. The poisonous timber rattlesnake is seldom seen above 5,000 feet, while the poisonous copperhead snake is rarely found above 2,500 feet.

There have never been any reported deaths due to a snake bite in the Park. Most snake bite kits are not effectively used. Your best precaution is to look before you step over logs and to avoid rock piles and old decayed buildings.

All snakes are protected by law in the Smokies, so hikers should not attempt to hurt them. Snakes are important in controlling the rodent populations in the Park.

There are only a few hundred (estimated 300-600) black bear in the Park and most are usually very shy of humans. Bear populations have increased in the Park since about 1989, but may have declined in the last year due to reduced mast (nut) crops. Over 70 bear had to be trapped and removed in 1989, compared to about 25 removals in most years. Most of these removals were from sites near car campgrounds.

Bear met on the trail will usually run away. I have encountered about eight bear during the day while hiking over 1,200 miles in the Smokies and they have all run from me. Rarely will you encounter a bear on the trail that has become fearless of humans.

If you encounter a more aggressive bear on the trail, do not run or play dead. Loud shouting will usually scare away most bear. Take extra precautions if the bear exhibits aggressive behavior such as snorting, false charges, teeth snapping, or swatting. In such an encounter, remember that bear are faster, stronger, and more agile than humans. And, never get between a bear and her cubs!

All food should be suspended from trees as recommended in Park literature. Hang your packs at least 10 feet from the nearest trees and 10 to 15 feet above the ground. Cook some distance (50 to 100) from your sleeping area and do not carry any food into your tent. Avoid cooking at dusk when bear are most actively foraging. Bear have an extremely well-developed sense of smell, so keep all food and trash in Ziploc bags and avoid highly scented soaps and perfumes in the backwoods!

Park rangers can inform you about the campsites that are more likely to attract bears. You can recognize campsites with bear problems by the frayed ropes left hanging from trees or the obvious claw marks along tree trunks. In these areas, I hang my food twice as high! Campsites with a persistent bear problem are occasionally closed for several weeks so the bear will stop associating the site with easy food. Report all bear incidents to park rangers.

The last animal of serious concern in the Park is the wild boar, which was accidentally established in the Park. They are extremely powerful and dangerous, but for the most part, they are nocturnal and usually timid.

Boar "sign" is commonly seen as rooted-up leaves and disturbed areas on the ground. If boar are encountered, quietly retreat, or if necessary, drop your pack and jump up the nearest tree!

All in all, the chances that you will have an ill-encounter in the Park with creatures of the woods are very small! My best advice is to treat all animals with great respect, and remember that you are the visitor to their homes and you are probably a greater threat to their health and safety than they are to yours.

Water

Purify all water in the backcountry! Waterborne parasites can cause severe diarrhea as well as long-term problems. The most well-known water contaminant is the paramecium Giardia (pronounced GEE-ar-dee-a), which can cause extreme stomach troubles and explosive diarrhea!

Most inexpensive water filters will not remove Giardia unless they filter out cysts smaller than forty microns. Chemical treatments are often not effective. Be sure to use fresh halazone or iodine tablets and allow sufficient purification time. If the water is murky with a lot of sediment, treat heavily and with regular shaking. The Park literature recommends boiling water for at least one minute at a hard boil—up to five minutes at high elevations!

Be sure to practice good personal hygiene and do not wash yourself, your clothes, or your cooking equipment directly in streams or ponds. Take wash water at least 100 feet from streams to wash. Use pit toilets where available or dig a shallow "cat-hole" at least 100 feet from the trail or any water sources. A cat-hole toilet is a shallow depression made with the heel of your boot or with a trowel. It is filled after use and usually covered with a small pile of rocks or rotten debris. Park regulations require that all feces be buried six inches deep. Deer have an insatiable desire for salt, so try to cover urine or urinate away from camp.

Etiquette and Ethics

We tourists need to be more environmentally responsible for our impact on the Park's resources. We have been careless stewards of this land and our love for the Smokies (nearly nine million automobile visitors during each of the last few years) has threatened the plants and animals. Our overuse of certain trails has resulted in deeply eroded footpaths and exposed tree roots. The ozone from our automobiles is believed to be a major factor in the decline of the high elevation spruce-fir forests.

The concepts of green tourism and low impact camping need to be expanded so that we lessen our impact on the Park's ecosystems. Green tourism involves reducing our impact on nature by choosing non-destructive or less-consumptive forms of tourism. Reduce the distance you travel to your recreation, and reuse, repair, and finally recycle your consumptive products and needs. Green tourism implies sustainable tourism and managing recreational use based on the carrying capacity of the resource. The overuse problem in certain camping areas has been addressed by the Park in their implementation of the rationed campsite system and increased publicity about alternative campsites. Campsite use is monitored and studied to determine if a backcountry area is being overused. The more heavily used campsites are rationed to restrict excessive use. Campsites are occasionally relocated and the old sites allowed to recover.

Campers can reduce their impact by practicing low impact camping techniques such as using backpacking stoves instead of campfires. If you build a campfire, make it small and only use dead, dry, downed wood. You really can collect small enough twigs and limbs so that you do not need to cut any wood.

Use only wood that you can break over your knee or stomp with your foot. Wood saws and axes are best left at home. Campfire rings should be small and removed prior to leaving the campsite. Do not leave any partially burnt logs at the site, and scatter ashes and unburnt wood amongst the vegetation.

Low impact camping is often called "no trace" camping. You should minimize your impact on the forest so that there is little disturbance and "sign" that you have even used the area. I highly recommend the book *Walking Softly in the Wilderness: The Sierra Club Guide to Backpacking* by John Hart (see Appendix B) for more extensive recommendations on how to reduce your impact on the ecosystems you so love to experience. If we do not protect these resources, we will lose them to overuse.

In addition to respecting Park regulations that are designed to make everyone (including animals) happier and healthier, I propose the following suggested "guidelines to good behavior." 1) "Do unto others as you would have them do unto you." 2) "Take only pictures, leave only footprints." 3) On narrow trails, yield the path to downhill hikers (they have lots of momentum) and yield the trail to uphill hikers (so they don't lose their momentum). In short, I suggest yielding the way to anyone (anything!) that wants the right-of-way. I generally greet people with a "hello," and if they seem inclined to stop and chat, I take the opportunity to share information and take a short break. 4) When you take a break, be sure to get well off the trail. 5) In campsites, try to camp away from your neighbor and respect their privacy. Keep noise to a minimum, especially after retirement to tents. Minimize walking through someone else's camp.

Behavior in shelters is probably my biggest complaint, and problems are worse if bad weather keeps you in close quarters. Keep your gear out of the way and do not block traffic to the door/gate. Keep common areas (around tables, etc.) clean and uncluttered. Once you finish cooking, move your gear so the next person can use the area. Keep the shelter gate closed, especially during mealtimes when bear and skunk may appear silently and in an instant! Dispose of waste water away from the shelter so as not to attract animals. Keep cooking fires to a minimum to reduce smoke and not waste limited firewood. Urinate well away from shelters so as not to attract salt-desperate animals, especially deer! Keep as quiet as possible when rising in the morning. If weather permits, do your early morning packing outside of the shelter. Let sleeping "dogs" lie!

Day Hiking

A trip to the Smokies is not complete without taking at least a couple of day hikes. Day hikes require good footwear, light snacks, and a sufficient supply of water (at least one quart of water per person for a half-day hike).

For me, the average hiking time on Park trails is about two miles per hour. Most groups take a little longer. Check weather conditions before you go, and always carry raingear because sudden afternoon thunderstorms can occur at anytime. If you are planning a day hike, I highly recommend the small, informative book on day hiking by

Carson Brewer, *Hiking in the Great Smokies* (see Appendix B).

In addition to the regular backcountry trails, the Park offers two additional types of hiking trails: Quiet Walkways and Nature Trails. The inexpensive pamphlet *Walks and Hikes* (available at visitor centers) is a wonderful guide to 51 trails and includes brief trail descriptions and difficulty ratings.

Quiet Walkways are easy and short, generally less than a half-mile. These short trails take hikers to the edges of the wilderness. At most of the trailheads, there are only a couple of parking spaces because overuse would mar the tranquility of the forest experience.

The Park has 11 self-guiding Nature Trails. Most are between a half-mile and two miles long. Trailside signs describe the natural history of the area. Nature Trails are generally more strenuous than Quiet Walkways and often have considerable elevation changes.

There are many waterfalls within the Park. Unfortunately, trails to all the easily accessible waterfalls are heavily used. Use caution when visiting waterfalls. The most dangerous activity for hikers involves climbing on rocks around waterfalls. Several people have fallen to their death as a result of climbing on slippery rocks near waterfalls.

Below is an equipment checklist with suggested items for a day hike. Feel free to customize and adapt this list.

Day Hike Equipment Checklist
❏ Day Pack
❏ Water Bottle
❏ Comfortable Shoes
❏ Map/Compass
❏ Food
❏ Camera
❏ Raingear
❏ First Aid Kit
❏ Flashlight
❏ Toilet Paper
❏ Emergency Kit

Five Favorite Day Hikes

The Smokies offer hundreds of day hikes. I have chosen five favorites from five different areas of the Park. The hikes range from 3 to 11 miles and represent the variety of day trips that can be enjoyed in the Park. You will experience extraordinary views and forests of huge trees as you hike some of the best day hikes in the Park.

Alum Cave Bluff Trail (31)

This 10-mile roundtrip hike is in the Mt. LeConte Area. The trail is the most heavily-used to the top of Mt. LeConte. The first section of the trail takes you through an extremely lush forest, and half-way to the summit, you will find Alum Cave, a massive overhang with a limited view and natural seating.

Most day hikers turn around here and miss the best part of this trail. Near the summit, there are marvelous views from narrow cliff-side trails with cable hand-holds. This is a strenuous hike if you go all the way to the summit.

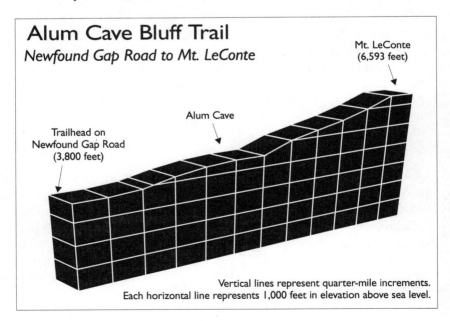

Alum Cave Bluff Trail
Newfound Gap Road to Mt. LeConte

Mt. LeConte
(6,593 feet)

Alum Cave

Trailhead on
Newfound Gap Road
(3,800 feet)

Vertical lines represent quarter-mile increments.
Each horizontal line represents 1,000 feet in elevation above sea level.

Gregory Ridge Trail (90)

This 11-mile roundtrip hike is in the Cades Cove Area. The trail leads through a dark primeval virgin forest and then ascends to the grassy summit of Gregory Bald, where you will find world-famous displays of flame azalea blooming from mid-June to July. A nearly 360-degree view offers excellent vistas to the east and southeast. *Note:* The first few miles of this trail make an enjoyable walk if you are not inclined to hike the longer, more strenuous part of this trail.

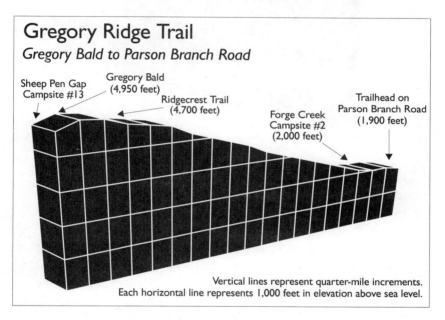

Gregory Ridge Trail
Gregory Bald to Parson Branch Road

Sheep Pen Gap
Campsite #13

Gregory Bald
(4,950 feet)

Ridgecrest Trail
(4,700 feet)

Forge Creek
Campsite #2
(2,000 feet)

Trailhead on
Parson Branch Road
(1,900 feet)

Vertical lines represent quarter-mile increments.
Each horizontal line represents 1,000 feet in elevation above sea level.

Forney Ridge Trail (107)

This 3-mile roundtrip is the easiest hike to one of the Park's mountain balds, Andrews Bald. The relatively easy trail begins at the parking area for Clingmans Dome and travels through thinning spruce and fir forest. The grassy summit of Andrews Bald offers excellent views north and south and makes a nice spot for a picnic.

Forney Ridge Trail
Clingmans Dome to Andrews Bald

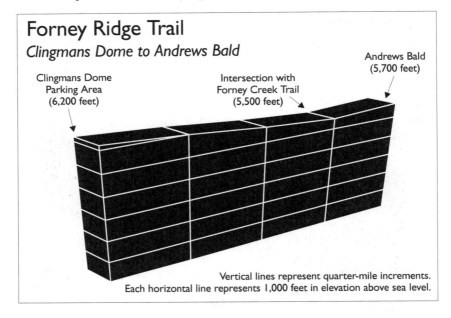

Clingmans Dome
Parking Area
(6,200 feet)

Intersection with
Forney Creek Trail
(5,500 feet)

Andrews Bald
(5,700 feet)

Vertical lines represent quarter-mile increments.
Each horizontal line represents 1,000 feet in elevation above sea level.

Gabes Mountain Trail (18)

This 7.8-mile hike is between the Greenbrier and Cosby Areas. The trail is accessed from the trailhead to Albright Grove (19) behind the Jellystone Campground on US 321 east of Gatlinburg. Hike this relatively easy trail if you want to experience the most amazing section of virgin forest in the Park.

You will transverse the lower slopes of the main ridge and pass through an area of virgin forest with record-sized beech, birch, maple, Frasir magnolia, and hemlock. The most impressive section of forest is found along the last mile east of the beautiful Sugar Cove Campsite #34.

Boogerman Trail (2)

This 7.5-mile hike is in the Cataloochee Area. From Cataloochee Campground, the trail follows rushing streams and loops up along a low ridge to an old farm site and by old stonewalls that disappear through the trees. Half-way into the loop, you will find a grove of huge tulip poplars. Do this loop counter-clockwise to enhance the mystery!

Gabes Mountain Trail
Maddron Bald to Cosby Campground

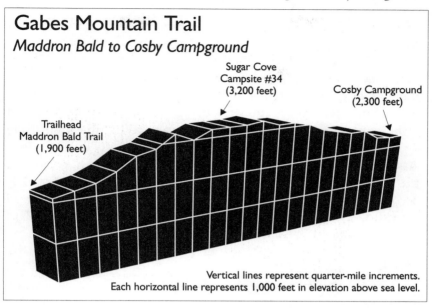

Sugar Cove
Campsite #34
(3,200 feet)

Cosby Campground
(2,300 feet)

Trailhead
Maddron Bald Trail
(1,900 feet)

Vertical lines represent quarter-mile increments.
Each horizontal line represents 1,000 feet in elevation above sea level.

Boogerman Trail
Cataloochee Road to Caldwell Fork Trail

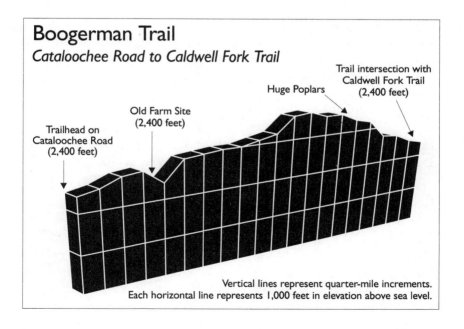

Trail intersection with
Caldwell Fork Trail
(2,400 feet)

Huge Poplars

Old Farm Site
(2,400 feet)

Trailhead on
Cataloochee Road
(2,400 feet)

Vertical lines represent quarter-mile increments.
Each horizontal line represents 1,000 feet in elevation above sea level.

Backpacking

My favorite times in the Park have occurred on multi-day trips. I find that it takes me about three days to get in rhythm with the wildness of the backcountry. I have written this book to be a "short course" to the Smokies, so I have included several books in Appendix B for more extensive information about backpacking equipment and techniques. I highly recommend that you purchase the new *Hiking Trails of the Smokies* by the Great Smoky Mountains Natural History Association. This book covers all the trails in the Park, providing trail details, water sources, and natural history. Each trail is accompanied by a profile map which helps hikers visualize trail difficulty. Trail descriptions by fifteen authors are provided with only minor inconsistencies about relative trail difficulty. Copies are widely available from camping stores or by mail from the GSMNHA.

I suggest that you consult topographical maps and make charts of the elevation changes of each mile on your particular trail. These will produce a "silhouette" or profile map that clearly shows the severity of elevation change and helps you plan the preferred direction of travel. I have included silhouette maps of the A.T. along the main ridge and my five favorite day hikes. These profiles hint at the physical exertion required along these sections.

A convenient scale for profile maps is a 5:1 vertical exaggeration. One mile on the horizontal axis should be the same length as 1,000 feet on the vertical axis. This scale is used on the silhouette maps in this book. If possible, do not plan major elevation changes early in your trip, when your pack is heaviest and you are not "broken-in" to the trail.

I generally plan to hike five to ten miles per day. Five to eight miles per day is even better! Increase or decrease the distance according to the amount of elevation change, the weight of your pack, and the physical condition and experience of your hiking partners. Hiking over eight to twelve miles is generally fatiguing and does not allow much time for camp chores or exploring.

I also prefer a "first-day-on-the-trail" distance of about three to five miles to allow a gradual introduction to the rigors of the trail.

Plan to be a bit sore, even if physically prepared, and carry aspirins or the equivalent to mute the soreness! My hiking partner swears by the use of additional calcium tablets to reduce bone soreness!

Carrying a small backpacking stove will vastly ease hot food preparation and reduce the depletion of the limited, local wood supply. If you must have campfires, please keep them small and use only "squaw wood." (Squaw wood—dead limbs and twigs found on the ground—was traditionally collected by Squaws. I have been able to find enough dry wood even during hurricanes, but I have not seen many Squaws!) Park regulations specify that you only use downed firewood. Standing dead trees are important to wildlife and should not be cut.

Wood that is wet on the outside but cleanly and loudly "snaps" when bent will burn. Sticks that bend or splinter irregularly are too wet or green to burn well. Dead pine, spruce, and fir contain flammable resins and burn quickly. Paper birch bark is another especially good fire starter. You can also "shave" damp wood to reach the dry center.

When planning trips, take special care to notice whether trails are marked "Hikers Only" or "Horses and Hikers." I find that most horse trails are heavily used and generally have more flies and unpleasant smells than non-horse trails. Horse backcountry campsites are also heavily used, buggier, smellier, and more likely to be "trashed" than non-horse sites. *Note:* Horses do not always "like" to pass hikers on trails. Yield the trail—step off into the brush or up the slope.

Backcountry camping is allowed at 18 shelters and nearly 100 designated backcountry sites. Most of the campsites are located near water. All shelters and 14 of the sites are rationed, meaning that reservations must be obtained and confirmed through the Backcountry Reservation Office.

Backcountry reservations for shelters and rationed sites can be obtained up to 30 days in advance. To register and get information on available space, call 423-436-1231 (8:30 A.M. to 6:00 P.M.), or write Backpacking Reservations, Great Smoky Mountains National Park, 107 Park Headquarters Road, Gatlinburg, TN 37738. Phone lines for reservations are usually busy, so let the phone ring until you are answered. Do not get frustrated if the lines are constantly busy. Someone will answer your call if you hold on long enough. You must reconfirm your reservation by phone by noon of the first day of your trip or the reservation will automatically be canceled.

All overnight camping requires self-issued backcountry use permits. These use permits must be completed by filling out a permit form and dropping copies into designated boxes at the visitor centers, campgrounds, or ranger stations. A copy of your permit must be presented to rangers in the backcountry when requested. Violators without proper permits are heavily fined and usually made to leave immediately.

The permits include the following information: 1) your name and the number of people in your party, 2) the campsite number(s) or trail shelter(s) name, 3) dates of use of the specific site (be prepared with one or two alternative campsites for each night), 4) where you plan to enter and exit the backcountry, and 5) the make and state license tag number of your car.

Individual group size is limited to eight. There is a three-day limit at each campsite and a one-day limit at any shelter. Generally, it can be a problem to get a specific campsite on weekends and holidays. It is also difficult to get space in shelters along the main ridge. Parties larger than four persons should make reservations two to four weeks in advance and have a list of alternative campsites.

The status of non-rationed sites is occasionally changed, so be sure to use a current map. I suggest a copy of *Great Smoky Mountains Trail Guide*, which can be purchased at the visitor centers ($.50) or by writing GSMNHA ($1 postpaid). The maps in this book are based on the Park's backcountry site numbering system, but I highly recommend that you purchase the *Trail Guide* because it has current regulations and suggestions printed on the backside.

On a backpacking trip, every item you take adds weight and must be considered carefully. Carry sufficient equipment to stay warm, dry, and comfortable. If you want or need it, carry it! Below I have include an equipment checklist, which recommends items needed for overnight trips in the Smokies. This is merely an outline but should serve as a basic list when preparing and packing.

Backpacking Equipment Checklist

Bed and Shelter
- ❏ Weather Shelter
   (Tent/Rainfly/Tarp/etc.)
- ❏ Sleeping Bag/Stuff Sack
- ❏ Foam Pad(s)
- ❏ Groundcloth

Haulage
- ❏ Pack and Frame
- ❏ Raincover
- ❏ Water Container/Waterbag
- ❏ Stuff Sacks
- ❏ Day Pack (when appropriate)
- ❏ Plastic Bags

Clothing
- ❏ Boots and Socks
- ❏ Extra Socks/Underwear
- ❏ Long Pants and Shirt
- ❏ Raingear
- ❏ Running Shorts
- ❏ Windshell/60-40
- ❏ Extra Shoes/Sneakers

Winter Clothing
- ❏ Polypropylene Top
   and Bottom
- ❏ Pile Jacket
- ❏ Headgear and Gloves
- ❏ Gators
- ❏ Wool Shirt
- ❏ Down/Pile Booties

Personal Gear
- ❏ Toilet Kit/Toothbrush/etc.
- ❏ Reading Materials
- ❏ Lip Balm
- ❏ Sunscreen/Skin Lotion
- ❏ Watch
- ❏ Medicine(s)

Kitchen
- ❏ Stove/Cook Kit
- ❏ Fuel Bottle
- ❏ Fire Starter/Lighter
- ❏ Personal Eating Tools
- ❏ Food/Stuff Sacks
- ❏ Spice Kit/Condiments
- ❏ Water Filter/Treatment
- ❏ Emergency Food
- ❏ Bowl/Cup/Plate

Other
- ❏ First Aid Kit
- ❏ Bug Dope
- ❏ Maps/Compass
- ❏ Notebook/Pencils
- ❏ Flashlight/Extra Batteries
- ❏ Camera/Extra Film
- ❏ Knife
- ❏ Binoculars
- ❏ Cord/Rope
- ❏ Repair Kit/Patch Kit

_____ Five Favorite Backpacking Trips

Backpacking possibilities in the Smokies are endless. I offer five of my favorite multi-day trips to help you get started. The trips are loops so no shuttling or hitchhiking is necessary. These multi-day trips cover 30 to 45 miles, an average of three to six nights in the backcountry. While many options exist, recommended campsites are provided to help you plan your trip.

Cataloochee-Spruce Mountain Loop

This five-night loop is about 37 miles long and uses Campsite #42, Laurel Gap Shelter, and Campsite #38, #39, and #41. The trailhead is at Polls Gap, located along the Heintooga Spur Road near Balsam Mountain Campground.

Follow Polls Gap/Spruce Mountain Trail (5) along a ridge with steady elevation increases. This trail, which is heavily used by horses and in dire need of waterbars, leads to the summit of Spruce Mountain, where a firetower once stood that offered a 360-view of the main ridge of the Smokies. By climbing a tree, you can gain a view almost as good as from the former firetower. Because many of the evergreen trees on the summit are dead, there are some good lookouts, especially in winter.

Balsam Mountain Trail (15) leads around the high ridges surrounding Cataloochee Valley to Laurel Gap. The Mount Sterling Ridge Trail (13) follows a high ridge with a few lookouts and a fantastic view from Mt. Sterling Firetower.

Backtrack to Pretty Hollow Gap and follow Pretty Hollow Gap Trail (14) down into Cataloochee Valley. While the lower and middle sections of Pretty Hollow Gap Trail are exceptionally beautiful, the upper section is heavily mired by horse traffic. Follow the road, Big Fork Ridge Trail (9) and Caldwell Fork Trail to see the Big Poplars. Cut over to Rough Fork Trail (4) to return to Polls Gap.

Raven Fork-Appalachian Trail-Balsam Mountain Loop

This five- or six-night loop leads 43 miles along high ridges and beautiful creek valleys and uses Campsite #48, Pecks Corner Shelter, Tricorner Knob Shelter, Laurel Gap Shelter, and Campsite #44 or #47, and #48. The trailhead is at Smokemont Campground.

Follow Bradley Fork Trail (127) to Chasteen Creek Trail (137), which ends on the crest of Hughes Ridge. Take Upper Hughes Ridge Trail (134) to the main ridge near Pecks Corner. From Pecks Corner, enjoy a moderately level, high altitude (elevation 6,000 feet) ridge and walk through spruce-fir forest along the A.T. to Tricorner Knob Shelter.

From the shelter, Balsam Mountain Trail (15), which is almost entirely level, leads to the lovely Laurel Gap Shelter. Continue along Balsam Mountain Trail and descend 2,900 feet in 2.5 miles on Beech Gap Trail (140) to Round Bottom. The last mile is extremely steep.

Ascend Hyatt Bald Trail (139) to reach McGhee Springs Campsite #44 or continue to Enloe Creek Campsite #47 on Hyatt Ridge Trail (135) and Enloe Creek Trail (138). (Because both campsites are extremely beautiful, I have difficulty recommending one over the other. If you have time, camp at both!) Take Enloe Creek Trail back to the crest of Hughes Ridge and follow Chasteen Creek Trail (137) and Bradley Fork Trail (127) back to Smokemont.

Cosby-Balsam Mountain Loop

This five-night, 34-mile loop combines lowland and high ridge trails and uses Campsite #34 and #29, Tricorner Knob Shelter, Laurel Gap Shelter, and Campsite #37. The trailhead is at Cosby Campground.

Follow Gabes Mountain Trail (18) past Henwallow Falls and along a magnificent old growth forest on the lower slope of Gabes Mountain. Pick up Maddron Bald Trail (19) and locate the side trail through Albright Grove, an exceptional area of huge yellow poplar trees.

Above the Grove, the trail leads to the A.T. on the main ridge. Follow the A.T. along the high ridge to Tricorner Knob and turn onto the Balsam Mountain Trail (15) to reach Laurel Gap Shelter. Backtrack to the beautiful Gunter Fork Trail (29) and go down to Walnut Bottoms. Take Low Gap Trail (27) and Cosby Creek/Low Gap Trail (22) back to Cosby Campground.

For a two-night, 17-mile loop, take Gabes Mountain Trail (18) and camp at Sugar Cove Campsite #34. Then follow Maddron Bald Trail (19) and camp at Otter Creek Campsite #29. Return to Cosby Campground on Snake Den Ridge Trail (20).

Greenbrier-Mt. LeConte Loop

This three-night, 32-mile loop is strenuous and uses Campsite #32 and #31, and Mt. LeConte Shelter. You will travel lowland trails through sections of old growth and climb the highest trail ascent in eastern North America to the summit of Mt. LeConte. The trailhead is at the Cherokee Orchard Parking Area.

Take Baskins Creek Trail (42) and Grapeyard Ridge Trail (41) to Greenbrier Cove. Then follow Porters Flat Trail (38) through old growth forest and camp at Porters Flat Campsite #31. Backtrack through inspiring hemlock, oak, and yellow poplars and take Brushy Mountain Trail (36) to Trillium Gap.

Follow Trillium Gap Trail (33) and rise 3,010 feet from Greenbrier Cove to Trillium Gap. Then wind up another 2,700 feet on the upper section of Trillium Gap Trail to the top of Mt. LeConte, the highest summit in the East. (Who said it would be easy!)

From the top of Mt. LeConte, enjoy incredible views. Two of the best views the Park has to offer are Clifftop (for sunsets) and Myrtle Point (for sunrises). You can almost see the entire Smokies Range from these two overlooks.

Several trails lead back to Cherokee Orchard. Rainbow Falls Trail (34) is the rockiest and probably most popular. Bullhead Trail (35) has less rocky walking, but it is longer and bypasses Rainbow Falls.

Gregory Bald-Rich Mountain Loop

This six-night, 45-mile loop uses Russell Field Shelter and Campsite #13, #14, #11, #5, and #6. You will hike both lowland and high ridge trails through a wide variety of vegetation. The trailhead is at Cades Cove Picnic Area.

Take Anthony Creek Trail (73), turn onto Russell Field Trail (74), and reach the A.T. and main ridge. Follow the A.T. along the high ridge to Doe Knob.

Hike Gregory Bald Trail (89) across the open grassy bald and enjoy a spectacular 360-view. The bald is world-famous for its display of flame azaleas the last two weeks of June. Gregory Bald Trail gradually descends connecting ridges to Hannah Mountain Trail (88), Scott Gap-Abrams Creek Connector Trail (85), and Hatcher

Mountain Trail (84). These trails lead along low ridges through stunted pine and oak forest between Cades Cove and Abrams Creek Areas.

Beard Cane Trail (78) descends into a marvelous, three-mile section of level footpath that follows Beard Cane Creek below Hatcher Mountain. From this fault valley, the trail climbs up to Ace Gap. Take Ace Gap Trail (79) and Rich Mountain Trail (76) along ridges around Cades Cove Valley and steadily climb east to reach an area of virgin forest near the crest of Rich Mountain. Follow the nearly-level trail across Rich Mountain and camp at Turkeypen Ridge Campsite #6. By following part of Rich Mountain Loop Trail (75), you will end up back near Cades Cove Picnic Area.

Overnight Trips

If you only have time for an overnight trip, here are five of my favorites. See Part III for more details on individual areas.

- In the Cataloochee Area, take Caldwell Fork Trail (3) to Caldwell Fork Campsite #41 (9.6 miles roundtrip).
- In the Cosby Area, take Gabes Mountain Trail (18) to Sugar Cove Campsite #34 (10 miles roundtrip).
- In the Greenbrier Area, take Porters Creek Trail (38) to Porters Flat Campsite #31 (7.4 miles roundtrip).
- In the Cades Cove Area, take Gregory Ridge Trail (90) to Forge Creek Campsite #12 (3 miles roundtrip).
- In the Bradley Fork Area, take Chasteen Creek Trail (137) to Upper Chasteen Campsite #48 (8.4 miles roundtrip).

3
Guide to Specific Areas

I have divided the Park trail system into ten different areas, primarily based on major watersheds: the Appalachian Trail, Cataloochee Area, Cosby-Big Creek Areas, Mt. LeConte-Greenbrier Areas, Elkmont-Tremont Areas, Cades Cove-Abrams Creek-Rich Mountain Areas, Twentymile Creek-Eagle Creek Areas, Middle Creeks Areas, Deep Creek Area, and Bradley Fork-Raven Fork-Straight Fork Areas.

In each area, the detailed information provided emphasizes road access, car-camping opportunities, general sites of interest, listing of individual trails, suggested day hikes, and suggested backpacking trips.

For each trail, difficulty, milage, and elevation gain is given. Trails are briefly described to help you select areas to explore. In the descriptions, I use the Park's campsite number—for example, Porters Flat Campsite #31. Trails are numbered in parentheses—for example, Bullhead Trail (35). For the most part, I use the trail names found on Park signs and the names used in the GSMNHA's *Hiking Trails of the Smokies* (see Appendix B).

I have classified the trails into four distinct types based on topography, vegetation, and mood: (1) high ridge trails, (2) low ridge trails, (3) creek headwater trails, and (4) lower creek trails. Any trail that does not fit into one of these classifications is generally noted as a lowland trail. Include at least one of each of these trail types on your trip so you can experience the full variety of the Park.

The high ridge trails are typified by most of the A.T. through the Park and include grass and heath balds, mixed deciduous and evergreen forests, occasional lookouts, and no major stream crossings. These trails often have limited water sources. The spruce and fir forests above 4,000 feet are evergreen islands in the southern sky and contain plants and animals typical of northern forests. These high trails are frequently "clouded in" and may be subject to high winds and severe thunderstorms. High ridge trails are heavily used in June, July, and August because of cooler summer temperatures.

The low ridge trails include most of the side ridge trails that connect the lowlands to the main ridge. Along these trails, there are several changes in forest vegetation type as elevations vary between 2,000 and 5,000 feet. Typically these trails offer only occasional views in summer and water sources are extremely variable. Trails with no or questionable availability of water are noted. Forney Ridge Trail (106) and Welch Ridge Trail (105) are good examples of this trail type. These trails offer some of the best variety of fall leaf colors.

Creek headwater trails consist primarily of trails along the upper slope beginnings of small streams. These trails offer lush and varied vegetation and plentiful water. Creek headwater trails are some of my favorite trails because each one is unique and distinctive in composition and mood. Plan on numerous creek crossings and wet feet when hiking these trails. Eagle Creek Trail (96) and Forney Creek Trail (106) are typical examples, and each requires a half-dozen or more creek crossings without footbridges.

The lower creek trails, such as lower Hazel Creek Trail (100) and Forney Creek (106), are generally along wide jeep roads or old railroad grades. Travel through these rich forests requires much "rock-hopping" and wading to cross the wide streams. These trails are especially loved by fishermen and offer the best variety of spring wildflowers. Unfortunately, these trails tend to be the buggiest in the summer. Often there are footbridges or larger jeep bridges across the lowermost sections of the wider streams.

Appalachian Trail

Seventy miles of the famous, 2,100-mile Appalachian Trail passes through the Park. The A.T. is the backbone of the Park's trail system and connects trails between the different areas. Highlights along the A.T. include northern spruce-fir forests and views from Shuckstack Firetower, Spence Field, Thunderhead, Clingmans Dome, Charlies Bunion, and Mt. Cammerer.

The A.T. is accessible by car only from three areas of the Park: the southwestern end off of NC 28 near Fontana Dam, the center at Newfound Gap on Clingmans Dome Road, and the eastern end in Davenport Gap on TN 32 near I-40.

The A.T. offers a series of three-sided, Adirondack-style shelters located approximately 6 to 8 miles apart. The shelters offer space for 12 persons (two shelters have space for 14) and are designed with two-level sleeping platforms. Most of the bunks in shelters along the A.T. in the Park have recently been converted to solid wood sleeping platforms that are far superior to the former torture-rack, fence-wire bunks!

An open dirt floor area in front, the common-use space, is generally about 20 to 25 feet wide and 10 feet deep. Each shelter, except Scott Gap and Rich Mountain, are enclosed by a chain-link bear fence.

Most shelters have a stone fireplace, but they are practically useless because the fireplaces usually do not draw well and shelters are heavily smoked-out. Fireplaces are also usually found full of half-burnt wood and garbage that discourages enthusiasm for food preparations. Campfire rings are often set up in front of shelters, but use of backpacking stoves is highly encouraged.

All the shelters on the A.T. are heavily used. Disadvantages of shelters include: bear problems, limited wood supplies, and often noisy "kids-will-be-kids" groups. Also, each shelter is full of cute, but highly active, mice that are especially entertaining after dusk. The mice do not eat much, but they will chew through pockets in search of food. I hang my small food sack from the rafters on a rope with a deadman guard and leave my backpack against the wall on the floor with all pockets open.

When hiking longer trips, I usually try to schedule one night in a shelter for about every three days on the trail. This gives me a break from my small and usually wet tent!

Trail Description

The A.T. enters the southwestern end of the Park after crossing Fontana Dam and traverses the length of the Park primarily along the main ridge from Doe Knob to Davenport Gap. The A.T. goes up and down many minor peaks along the western ridge prior to climbing Clingmans Dome, and then descends to Newfound Gap, which can be considered the relative center of the A.T. in the Park. Thereafter, the A.T. follows a more level high ridge to the eastern end of the Park and includes a long descent before leaving the Park's boundary.

Especially strenuous sections in the western half of the A.T. through the Park include the climb from Fontana Dam to Shuckstack Firetower, Birch Spring Shelter to Doe Knob, Ekaneetlee Gap to Mollies Ridge, and the descent from Thunderhead to Beechnut Gap. Also, the decline from Sugar Tree Gap, just west of Derrick Knob

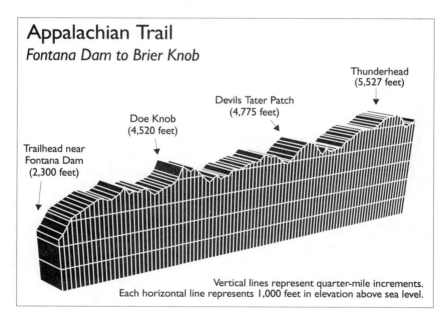

Appalachian Trail

Fontana Dam to Brier Knob

Thunderhead
(5,527 feet)

Devils Tater Patch
(4,775 feet)

Doe Knob
(4,520 feet)

Trailhead near
Fontana Dam
(2,300 feet)

Vertical lines represent quarter-mile increments.
Each horizontal line represents 1,000 feet in elevation above sea level.

Shelter, is a heck-of-a-climb if you are headed west, and the 2-mile stretch from Double Springs Gap to Clingmans Dome is a steady, strenuous climb.

The most strenuous sections in the eastern half of the Appalachian Trail through the Park include the climb from Chapman Gap to Mt. Chapman and down to Tricorner Knob Shelter, the long descent from Mt. Guyot to Camel Gap, the descent from Cosby Knob Shelter to Low Gap and climb to Mt. Cammerer Spur Trail, and the final 5-mile, 3,000-foot descent to the Park's boundary at Davenport Gap.

The Appalachian Trail (1)

This trail enters the Park along the top of Fontana Dam. The Fontana Dam Visitor Center offers free, hot-water showers in the outside restrooms and an interesting movie and tour of the tallest dam (height 480 feet) in the East. There is a restricted-use shelter for long-distance A.T. hikers near the dam and a popular ice cream store at nearby Fontana Village.

Park rangers are often available during the summer months to

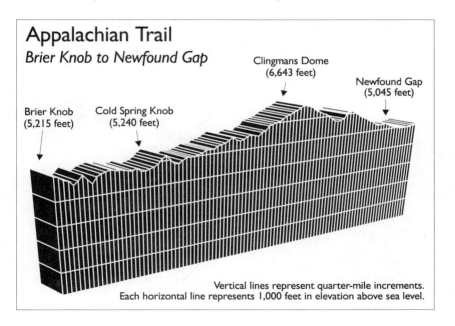

Appalachian Trail

Brier Knob to Newfound Gap

Clingmans Dome
(6,643 feet)

Newfound Gap
(5,045 feet)

Brier Knob
(5,215 feet)

Cold Spring Knob
(5,240 feet)

Vertical lines represent quarter-mile increments.
Each horizontal line represents 1,000 feet in elevation above sea level.

provide information and assistance in obtaining camping permits. The nearest ranger station is at Twentymile Creek, about 9 miles west of the dam.

Before the completion of Fontana Dam, which made crossing the Little Tennessee River much easier, the former route of the A.T. followed the main ridge west from Doe Knob for about 3 miles, where the main ridge trail now terminates at Gregory and Parson Balds. Trailside damage of vegetation and soil caused by the up-rooting habits of introduced, European boar is especially evident from here east to Newfound Gap. Problems with bear and salt-desperate deer are common at the beautiful Sheep Pen Gap Campsite #13, which is located just below Gregory Bald.

The A.T. climbs steeply from Fontana Dam (approximate elevation 1,900 feet) to the firetower on Shuckstack (elevation 4,020 feet). This 2,000-foot gain is over 3.5 miles. From the Birch Spring Gap Shelter, the trail gains another 600 feet to join the main ridge at Doe Knob (elevation 4,500 feet).

The A.T. passes through numerous small gaps and over peaks on its way to Clingmans Dome (elevation 6,643 feet), the highest

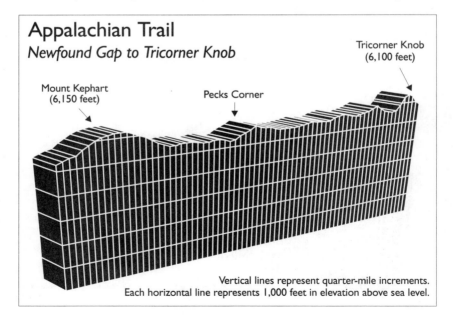

Appalachian Trail
Newfound Gap to Tricorner Knob

Tricorner Knob
(6,100 feet)

Mount Kephart
(6,150 feet)

Pecks Corner

Vertical lines represent quarter-mile increments.
Each horizontal line represents 1,000 feet in elevation above sea level.

peak in the Park. Clingmans Dome Parking Area is located at the end of a 12-mile side road off Newfound Gap Road. Clingmans Dome Tower is a massive concrete-ramp lookout tower that is accessible by foot at the end of a .5-mile path. The summit of Clingmans Dome is often clouded-in, and the best views are generally obtained in late fall and early winter, especially in early morning or following major thunderstorms.

Beyond Newfound Gap, the A.T. steadily ascends the ridge northeast to Icewater Spring Shelter. This section of trail is one of the busiest in the Park because a lot of day hikers and backpackers start their trip at Newfound Gap.

Beyond Icewater Spring Shelter, the trail follows a winding and narrow, knife-edge ridge where there are numerous impressive views primarily to the west and north. There are spectacular views from Charlies Bunion and along the narrow trail to Tricorner Knob.

The A.T. then follows the now broader ridge and climbs gradually around Mt. Guyot to Mt. Cammerer, the last and most eastern prominent peak on the A.T. in the Park. A short trail, Mt. Cammerer Side Trail (23), leads to a boarded-up stone tower on the summit

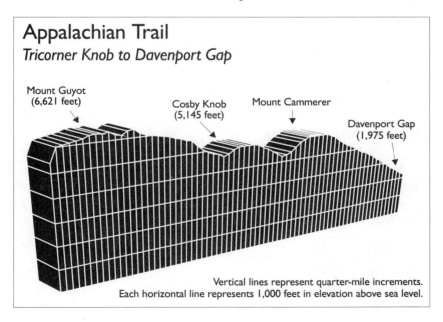

Appalachian Trail
Tricorner Knob to Davenport Gap

Mount Guyot
(6,621 feet)

Cosby Knob
(5,145 feet)

Mount Cammerer

Davenport Gap
(1,975 feet)

Vertical lines represent quarter-mile increments.
Each horizontal line represents 1,000 feet in elevation above sea level.

Appalachian Trail Shelters

Shelter	Elevation	Use	Hikers	Horses	Comments
Birch Spring Gap	3680	RS	12	12	Trashy/ Muddy
Mollies Ridge	4570	RS	12	12	Heavy Use
Russell Field	4360	RS	14	14	Heavy Use
Spence Field	4900	RS	12	12	Bears/Trashy
Derrick Knob	4890	RS	12	None	Heavy Use
Silers Bald	5460	RS	12	12	Small Bald
Double Springs	5507	RS	12	None	Heavy Use
Ice Water Springs	5920	RS	12	None	Heavy Use
Pecks Corner	5280	RS	12	12	Nice Forest
Tricorner Knob	5920	RS	12	None	Trashy
Cosby Knob	4700	RS	12	12	Limited View
Davenport Gap	2600	RS	12	12	Heavy Use

of Mt. Cammerer where there are usually fantastic views in all directions.

The A.T. descends steadily for 4 miles to the northeastern end of the Park at Davenport Gap and TN 32. From here, the A.T. drops another 1,000 feet to the bridge crossing Big Pigeon River and adjacent to I-40. Cars parked at Davenport Gap are subject to break-in; the safest parking is at the Big Creek Ranger Station, which is over 1 mile away by road. Chestnut Branch Trail (26) leads from the A.T. to the ranger station.

Recommended Hiking

Day hikes on the A.T. are easiest from the two trailheads where the A.T. enters the Park, from points along the Clingmans Dome Road, and from the Newfound Gap Parking Area. Day hikes from Clingmans Dome Road and Newfound Gap require less elevation gain. Although demanding, the 8-mile roundtrip hike along the A.T. from Newfound Gap to Charlies Bunion is very popular.

Cataloochee Valley

Cataloochee Valley is one of my favorite areas of the Park because of its great beauty and extensive trail system. It is less heavily used compared to most areas of the Park. The valley contains wonderful sections of virgin forest, lovely streams, and numerous historical buildings and demonstrations.

Cataloochee Valley was heavily settled by the mid-1800s and remained a self-contained community until the 1930s when the land was condemned for the formation of the Park. The valley's rich human history is still remembered in the weathered boards of reconstructed churches, schools, and remaining home sites with aged rock chimneys and rock walls.

Cataloochee Valley, located on the southeastern end of the Park is far from the main tourist traffic and is only accessible along a fairly narrow gravel road that is not recommended for RV's. The easiest access is from the intersection of I-40 and NC 276, northeast of Maggie Valley, North Carolina.

Follow Cove Creek Road (County Road 1395) to the Park's boundary at Cove Creek Gap (where it turns to gravel) and continue 4 miles to a paved road that leads to the primitive Cataloochee Campground and Ranger Station. The gravel Cataloochee-Big Creek Road continues along the eastern edge of the Park to the Big Creek Area and access to I-40 at the Waterville Exit.

Camping is available at Cataloochee Campground, which is frequently filled on weekends. This small, but very pleasant, campground contains 30 sites, making it an excellent base camp for day hiking. The nearest private campgrounds are along Jonathan Creek (NC 276) and in Maggie Valley.

Trail Descriptions

Two main trails, Caldwell Fork (3) and Rough Fork (4), generally run parallel to each other through the central part of the valley. Several connector trails join the two main trails with the surrounding "rim" trails along the bordering ridges.

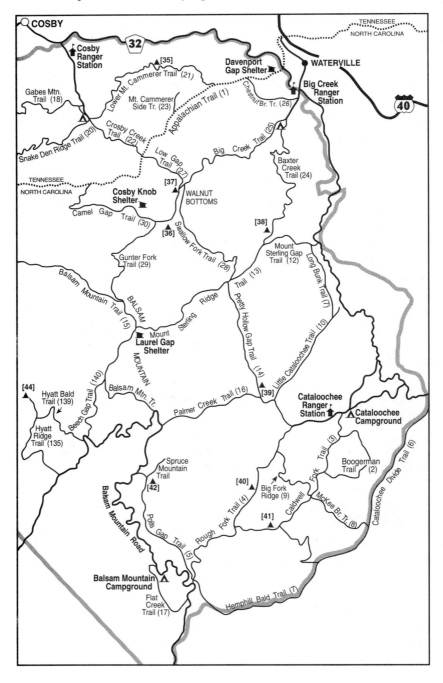

The trails in the valley floor are mostly old roadbeds and are generally well-graded. The trails along the small streams are especially lush and beautiful.

Boogerman Trail (2)

This moderate, 4-mile trail has an elevation gain of only 900 feet. It is well-known for the variety of magnificent-sized trees. Do not miss this trail!

The trailhead is on Caldwell Fork Trail (3). After leaving Caldwell Fork, the trail ascends a low ridge to a gap, slabs (runs across the mountain slope with only gradual elevation change) the mountainside with only two additional short climbs, reaches a side ridge, and descends back to Caldwell Fork. It is best to do this trail as a day hike from Cataloochee Campground, a 7.5-mile roundtrip.

Caldwell Fork Trail (3)

This moderate lower creek trail gains 1,300 feet in elevation. It follows a rushing mountain stream for nearly 5 miles and there are log footbridges at every stream crossing.

While any section would be suitable for a day hike, the trail is heavily used by horses and is mired in several spots. The prettiest sections are on Boogerman Trail (2) or at the upper end of the trail near the three exceptionally large "Big Poplars," which are believed to be the among the largest yellow poplars in the Park. The largest of the three requires the outstretched and connected arms of six people to encircle the trunk, which is eight feet in diameter.

Rough Fork Trail (4)

This 6.5-mile lower creek trail begins by following a stream along a gravel road for a couple of miles and then passes several restored farm houses. The middle section of the trail becomes a narrow footpath, travels through impressive forest to a side ridge, and follows a wide railroad grade for several miles to Polls Gap (indicated on older maps as Paul's Gap). The trail near Polls Gap is very gradual and makes a wonderful, short day hike. There is no water after Campsite #40.

Spruce Mountain Trail (5)

This high ridge trail is deeply rutted due to overuse by horses. It is moderate in difficulty with an elevation change of only 800 feet. The trail follows the ridge from Polls Gap for 5.5 miles towards the summit of Spruce Mountain with a climb into a declining evergreen forest at Spruce Mountain Campsite #42. The view from the nearby Spruce Mountain Firetower (now removed) was once one of the best in the Park.

Cataloochee Divide Trail (6)

This moderate trail gains nearly 1,500 feet in 6.5 miles. The trail travels east with a few major climbs from Double Gap just below Hemphill Bald to Cove Creek Gap at the junction with Cove Creek Road and Cataloochee Road.

This is a nice hike in a high ridge forest with a few good lookouts (best in winter) but no dependable water sources. This trail is most suitable for a day hike from Cove Creek Road or the private "The Swag" retreat at the head of Hemphill Bald Road.

Hemphill Bald/Double Gap Trail (7)

This moderate low ridge trail ascends 1,800 feet in 8.5 miles. The trail starts fairly level at Polls Gap but begins to climb steeply on switchbacks after Maggot Spring and until Hemphill Bald.

There are several superb lookouts, most notably a view east from Hemphill Bald. The bald was named after a pioneer family. This trail is used extensively by horses but is generally in good condition. There are few water sources along this ridge, the most reliable is a strong spring about 1 mile east of Polls Gap.

McKee Branch Trail (8)

This creek headwater trail ascends 2.3 miles from Caldwell Fork to Cataloochee Divide, which includes a 1,700-foot climb to the ridge. This trail is extremely strenuous and very steep in sections. There are some pretty stands of forest along this trail, but there are no dependable water sources after the second stream crossing.

Cataloochee Backcountry Campsites

Campsite	Number	Elevation	Use	Hikers	Horses
Pretty Hollow	39	3040	Medium	20	20
Big Hemlock	40	3100	Light	10	Yes
Caldwell Fork	41	3360	Light	10	Yes
Spruce Mtn.	42	5480	Light	10	Yes
Laurel Gap Shelter		5600	Medium	14	Yes

Big Fork Ridge Trail (9)
This low ridge trail links Caldwell Fork and Rough Fork in the middle of Cataloochee Valley. Crossing the low ridge separating these two parallel creeks and trails, you will hike a moderate, 3-mile stretch. This trail can be used for day hikes or as part of a longer loop.

Little Cataloochee Trail (10)
This moderate lowland trail gains only 900 feet in over 5 miles. The trailheads are at Palmer Creek, about 1 mile from the end of the paved section of Cataloochee Road at the Cataloochee Horse Camp, and at a signed gate along the gravel Cataloochee-Big Creek Road.

The trail follows old roads with only one notable climb over the small ridge that separates the two Cataloochees. There are plenty of water sources and several old home sites where only rock foundations or chimneys remain. A restored church in Little Cataloochee has an interesting cemetery on the ridge slope below. This church is still used for occasional services and family reunions.

Long Bunk Trail (11)
This relatively strenuous lowland trail climbs 900 feet in nearly 3.7 miles between Little Cataloochee and Mt. Sterling Gap Trail. The trail winds around and over minor low ridges, travels through a couple of small, narrow valleys, and passes by several old farm sites. There is an especially beautiful valley and farm site about 1 mile from the northern end of the trail. This shady trail makes a very pleasant hike on a hot summer afternoon because cool air flows down from the high slopes above.

Mount Sterling Gap Trail (12)

This low ridge trail begins at Mt. Sterling Gap on Cataloochee-Big Creek Road. It is rated extremely strenuous because of a 2,000-foot climb in 2.3 miles along an old jeep trail to a ridge .5 miles below the Mt. Sterling Firetower. This firetower is one of three remaining in the Park.

There are several excellent lookouts from the trail prior to reaching the main ridge, but the view from the tower is unequalled in the Park. The view includes the Pigeon River Gorge (below), the Unaka Mountains, the main ridge of the Smokies, the Black Mountains (east), and the end of the Southern Appalachians.

Mt. Sterling Ridge Trail (13)

This moderate high ridge trail descends 900 hundred feet over 6 miles. The descent is steady from the Mt. Sterling Firetower to Pretty Hollow Gap. The trail climbs steeply out of the gap and follows the relatively level ridge to Laurel Gap along Big Cataloochee Mountain. *Note:* The campsite near here (Mt. Sterling Campsite #38) is heavily used and there always seems to be a resident bear nearby. The campsite has been recently moved away from the firetower and closer to the water source. If you climb Baxter Creek Trail (24) from Big Creek to Mt. Sterling, the side trail to the water source is about .25 miles from the summit.

Pretty Hollow Gap Trail (14)

This strenuous creek headwater trail is 5 miles long and rises 2,300 feet, connecting Cataloochee Valley and Mt. Sterling Ridge. The lower end of the trail follows the beautiful Pretty Hollow Creek, which is easily viewed from the old roadway. You will have to cross the stream several times and there are no bridges at two of the crossings.

There is a magnificent stand of huge hemlock at the last crossing (a log bridge), about 3 miles from the trailhead on Cataloochee Road. I am told there is a fantastic section of virgin forest up Cook's Creek, but the only trail is a rough fisherman's path.

After that last stream crossing, the trail becomes very muddy.

There are several 100-yard sections of deep mud that must be conquered before reaching the gap.

Balsam Mountain Trail (15)

This moderate high ridge trail only gains 1,600 feet in about 11 miles. The northern half of the trail is easy. The gorgeous path leads through evergreen spruce-fir forest from the A.T. at Tricorner Knob to Laurel Gap Shelter. The shelter, which is located at the site of an old logging camp, has abundant water nearby, but this is the only dependable water source on the trail. The southern half of this trail follows along old railroad grades to connect with Balsam Mountain Road and the nearby Palmer Creek Trail (16).

Palmer Creek Trail (16)

This strenuous creek headwater trail gains nearly 1,800 feet in its 3.3 miles from Cataloochee Valley to Balsam Mountain Road. The trail is heavily used by horses. *Note:* Balsam Mountain Trail (15) is about .3 miles to the north along the Balsam Mountain Road (gravel).

The trail follows Palmer Creek for about half its length and then climbs more steeply along a narrow side ridge to Pin Oak Gap on Balsam Mountain. Near the gap, the trail passes through a thick patch of evergreen ground cover—galax—which has a distinct odor of moldy leaves.

Flat Creek Trail (17)

This trail is isolated from other trails around the Balsam Mountain Area, but it is exceptionally beautiful and makes a wonderful day hike. This creek headwater trail is moderate in difficulty, descending 400 feet in 2.5 miles.

The trail begins near Balsam Mountain Campground at the Heintooga Picnic Area, where there is an outstanding lookout at the far end of the grounds. Following Flat Creek through open grassy forest, a gradual, almost level, path leads 2 miles to Flat Creek Falls and a view of the middle ridge of the Smoky Mountains.

A short side trail, which is steep and slippery, leads down to the top of the falls. Most of the year (except winter), the view from the top of the falls is obscured by vegetation. The best view of the falls is from Heintooga Ridge Road, across the valley near the trailhead.

The last mile of the Flat Creek Trail is slightly more strenuous. The trail goes up and over a 300-foot ridge to a pretty creek and then climbs steeply up to a trailhead on Heintooga Ridge Road.

You can arrange to have cars at either trailhead, but I recommend hiking down to the falls from Heintooga Picnic Area and then wandering back through the grassy park-like Flat Creek Valley. *Note:* Heintooga Road is usually gated several miles south of the picnic area in the winter.

Recommended Hikes

Recommended day hikes in the area include Boogerman Trail (2), Hemphill/Double Gap Trail (7), Long Bunk Trail (11), Mt. Sterling Gap Trail (12), and Pretty Hollow Gap Trail (14). Two highly recommended day hikes (which also could be overnighters) involve hiking into Big Hemlock Campsite #40 on Rough Fork Trail (4) or into Caldwell Fork Campsite #41 on Caldwell Fork Trail (3).

Big Hemlock Campsite is located in a grove of huge hemlocks, usually a dark, cool, and moist place. In recent years, several large hemlocks have died and the area is more open, brighter, and less primeval. Caldwell Fork Campsite is located in a small half-open valley near the "Big Poplars."

Numerous longer loops can also be made in this area. The loop from Cataloochee Campground (or the end of the paved road) to Spruce Mountain Campsite #42 and along Balsam Mountain is especially gorgeous. Or, go to Spruce Mountain and back to Cataloochee Valley (use trail 13, 15, 5, and 4).

The loop from Polls Gap around the rim of Cataloochee Valley to Hemphill Bald offers impressive views to the north and east. From Hemphill Bald and Cataloochee Divide, several side trails (7, 8, or 4) lead down to Cataloochee Valley and back to Polls Gap. Another recommended loop in the Cataloochee Valley Area goes to Mt. Sterling Firetower (use trail 14 and 13) and then returns to Cataloochee (use trail 12, 11, and 10).

Cosby-Big Creek Areas

Two highly favored areas in the Smokies are Cosby and Big Creek drainages, which lie in the moist, northeast end of the Park. Area highlights include the trail from Big Creek Campground to Walnut Bottoms, side trails to the main ridge and to Mt. Sterling, virgin forest at Albright Grove and along Gabes Mountain, and the superb views from Mt. Cammerer. In the Cosby Area, hemlock trees grow all along the lower northern slopes, whereas in other areas of the Smokies, hemlock more commonly grow in wet ravines and along streams.

The Cosby Area is most easily reached from I-40 and US 321 east of Gatlinburg, Tennessee. A short section of the Foothills Parkway connects I-40 with Cosby, Tennessee. The Cosby Area is located just off TN 32 a few miles from the community of Cosby. This area includes a ranger station and campground.

Cosby Campground is not usually full because it is many miles from the main tourist areas around Gatlinburg. The campground is one of the prettiest in the Park because the clever layout of the campsites allows more isolation and privacy. There are several private campgrounds just outside the Park near Cosby and along US 321 towards Gatlinburg.

TN 32 continues along the edge of the Park to the Big Creek Area. Signs are posted to lead you upstream along the Pigeon River to Walters Power Plant and beyond into the Big Creek Area.

Big Creek Area has a ranger station and a primitive campground. In late 1993, the campground and horse-access area underwent extensive improvements, which included new bathrooms and parking areas.

Trail Descriptions

In the Cosby-Big Creek Areas, five trails leave from Cosby Campground: Gabes Mountain Trail (18), Maddron Bald Trail (19), Snake Den Ridge Trail (20), Lower Mt. Cammerer Trail (21), and Cosby Creek/Low Gap Trail (22). Three trails leave from Big Creek Ranger Station: Baxter Creek Trail (24), Big Creek Trail (25), and Chestnut Branch Trail (26).

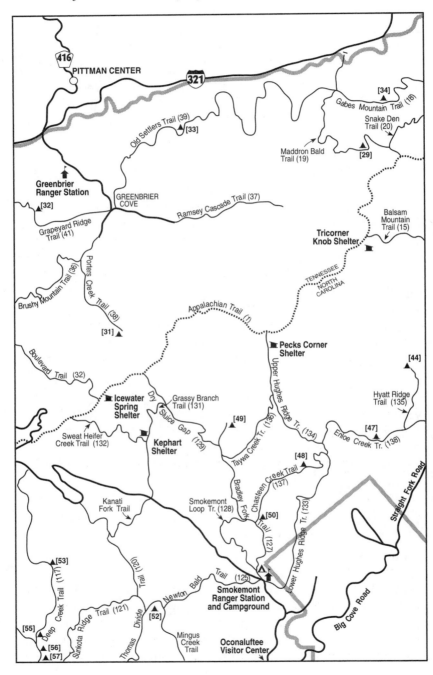

Gabes Mountain Trail (18)

This 6.6 mile trail links Cosby Campground with Maddron Bald Trail (19) and Old Settlers Trail (39) and passes through one of the prettiest sections of forest in the Park (See Five Favorite Day Hikes section for more details). A 1.2-mile approach trail leads to the western trailhead from the parking area off of Laurel Springs Road (Hwy. 321).

Maddron Bald Trail (19)

This lowland trail follows a jeep road and leads to Albright Grove, a well-known area of preserved old growth forest. The trail becomes a low ridge trail along its upper end above Otter Creek Campsite #29. The trail is moderately difficult, rising 2,600 feet in 7 miles.

The trailhead is partially hidden on Laurel Springs Road, which loops behind the private Jellystone Campground on US 321 east of Gatlinburg. This road is about 3 miles west of Cosby and 15.5 miles east of Gatlinburg.

From the trailhead, the jeep road leads 3 miles, with about 1,500 feet of elevation gain, to a short loop trail through Albright Grove. While the Grove contains some magnificent poplars, I personally feel that Gabes Mountain Trail passes through a much better example of virgin forest.

From the Grove, the trail narrows and continues upward to Otter Creek Campsite #29, about 1 mile away. This rationed campsite has a reputation for bear incidents and is occasionally closed. Be sure to use the unique pack- and food-hanging cable provided.

About 1 mile from the lower trailhead, locate the ends of Gabes Mountain Trail (18) and Old Settlers Trail (39). From the ridge at the end of Maddron Bald Trail, you can continue along a connector trail for .7 miles to the A.T. or take Snake Den Trail (20) back to Cosby Campground to complete a loop.

Snake Den Ridge Trail (20)

This low ridge trail is extremely strenuous, descending 3,400 feet in 4.5 miles. The trail follows a wide jeep road along the ridge and drops down steeply along a side ridge, where there are a couple of superb views. Then the trail curves off the ridge and passes through some beautiful hardwood forest near the end of the trail at Cosby Campground. This trail would make a nice, but extremely tough, day

Cosby-Big Creek Backcountry Campsites

Campsite	Number	Elevation	Use	Hikers	Horses
Otter Creek	29	4560	Medium	10	No
Sugar Cove	34	3240	Medium	15	No
Gilliland Creek	35	2680	Medium	15	8
Upper Walnut Bottoms	36	3040	Rationed	20	No
Lower Walnut Bottoms	37	3000	Rationed	20	No
Mount Sterling	38	5820	Rationed	20	No
Pretty Hollow	39	3040	Medium	20	20
Davenport Gap Shelter		2600	Rationed	12	Yes

hike. Consider hiking from the campground to the fine view from the first ridge and back. *Note:* There are no water sources along the upper half of this trail.

Lower Mt. Cammerer Trail (21)

Most of this moderate path is a lowland trail. It rises 1,300 feet in 7.5 miles. Beginning at Cosby Campground, the trail wraps around the slopes of Mt. Cammerer and ends at the A.T. The first part of this trail makes a great day hike.

There are few views along this trail. The best view is from Sutton Ridge, which is about 1.5 miles from Cosby Campground. This makes a great day hike. And, the 2 miles before the A.T. are especially beautiful, crossing several creeks with small waterfalls.

Cosby Creek/Low Gap Trail (22)

This extremely strenuous, 2.5-mile trail rises 1,800 feet from Cosby Campground to Low Gap. Near the campground, the trail passes through a gorgeous, dark forest with lush ferns and mosses, then the trail climbs steadily along a wide trail with several switchbacks and reaches the A.T. at Low Gap.

A steep ascent out of Low Gap along the A.T. takes you to Cosby Knob Shelter, about .8 miles away. Also, I highly recommended hiking from Low Gap to Mt. Cammerer, which is about 3 miles east.

Mt. Cammerer Side Trail (23)

This easy high ridge trail begins on the A.T. and the first part is nearly level, rising only 1,700 feet in a little over .5 miles. Your destination is the old Mt. Cammerer Lookout Tower. The massive rock tower was boarded-up in the late 1980s because it had been heavily damaged. There has been interest in re-opening the tower.

While reaching the trailhead on the A.T. is strenuous, the superb views from the base of the tower make the hike worth the effort. The tower may be in clouds when the rest of the area isn't, but on a clear day, you can see in all directions.

Baxter Creek Trail (24)

This 6-mile low ridge trail is exceedingly beautiful, ascending through several forest types and emerging into an evergreen spruce forest carpeted by thick mosses and clumps of ferns on the summit of Mt. Sterling. While this trail is quite strenuous, it is a more gradual route to the summit of Mt. Sterling than Mt. Sterling Gap Trail (12).

Big Creek Trail (25)

This moderate lower creek trail serves as the central link for the trails in the Big Creek Area. It climbs 1,300 feet in 5 miles to campsites at Walnut Bottoms. Lower Walnut Bottoms Campsite #37 is one of the most heavily used backcountry campsites in the Park, so call early for reservations. Bear-proof footlockers have been installed for storing food because this site has the worst reputation for bear incidents. Located in a wide valley next to the river, this campsite makes a great base camp for day hikes on side trails to the surrounding ridges. *Note:* Upper Walnut Bottoms Campsite #36, a horse camp, is about .25 miles upstream.

The Big Creek Trail is entirely along a wide gravel road. While the gravel is somewhat hard on the feet, the trail is gradual as it follows the beautiful Big Creek. There are bridges at every river crossing, so you do not have to get your feet wet, and there is a beautiful swimming hole about 1 mile from the trailhead.

Chestnut Branch Trail (26)

This strenuous, 2-mile trail descends 1,100 feet. From the A.T., the trail drops steadily through a lovely valley and reaches a side creek, then the trail remains close to the creek, passes several old homesites, and arrives at Big Creek Ranger Station.

Low Gap Trail (27)

This beautiful, but strenuous, lowland trail climbs 1,200 feet in 2.3 miles to reach the A.T. at Low Gap. The lower end of this trail does a big switchback out of Walnut Bottoms and offers numerous views of Big Creek. Then the trail leads gradually up through a small, but more open, valley and winds up the ridge into thick forest.

Swallow Fork Trail (28)

This strenuous creek headwater trail climbs steadily for nearly 2,200 feet in 4 miles. It leads gradually up the ridge through several small coves and then uses switchbacks to climb the steep ridge to Pretty Hollow Gap.

I find this trail to be one of the most beautiful in the Park and it is my favorite trail from Walnut Bottoms. Unfortunately, the trail is heavily mired in places by excessive horse travel.

Gunter Fork Trail (29)

This strenuous creek headwater trail leads from Walnut Bottoms to Balsam Mountain Trail (15), an ascent of 2,400 feet in 4 miles. The trail begins by following Gunter Fork for a couple of miles before turning up a side stream to a beautiful, 200-foot waterfall, and then climbs steadily to its destination in a gorgeous, green spruce-fir forest. The ground and lower tree trunks are completely covered by mosses, ferns, and an endless carpet of wood sorrel.

There are signs posted at each end of this trail that warn of dangerous stream crossings during periods of high water. The most dangerous stream crossing is at the trailhead near Walnut Bottoms. If there have been heavy rains recently, use the Swallow Fork Trail to reach Mt. Sterling and Balsam Mountain. *Note:* Above the falls, there are no dependable water sources.

Camel Gap Trail (30)

This moderate trail 0.9 miles south of Walnut Bottoms campsite (#37) climbs 1,600 feet in 4.1 miles. It follows an old railroad grade to Camel Gap on the A.T. The trail runs beside the river for several miles before winding around the valley to the ridge where it again meets the A.T.

Snake Den (20) and Maddron Bald (19) Trails, which lead into the Cosby Area, are about 3 miles west along the A.T. at the end of a .7-mile connector trail. From the connector trail, the Cosby Knob Shelter is about 1.5 miles east along the A.T.—the hike is very steep.

Recommended Hiking

Recommended day hikes in this area include Gabes Mountain Trail (18), Maddron Bald Trail (19), Baxter Creek Trail (24), and Big Creek Trail (25).

The short connector trails between the major ridges and creeks are some of the most beautiful trails in the Park. They pass through a variety of vegetation zones and highlight the variability found in the Park.

Swallow Fork Trail (28) to Pretty Hollow Gap is incredibly beautiful even though the upper third is mired by horse traffic. This is one of my favorite connector trails, and it led me to promise myself that I would eventually hike every trail in the Park!

Just west of Pretty Hollow Gap along Mount Sterling Ridge Trail (13), there is a beautiful spruce-sedge plant community, very lush with an open, park-like atmosphere. Here, dark-green spruce trees stand as scattered individuals in a sea of paler green, underlying sedge-grass that is highlighted by patches of sunlight.

_____Mt. LeConte-Greenbrier Areas

Mt. LeConte and Greenbrier are grouped together because of their proximity and interconnecting trail system. These areas are best known for beautiful spring wildflowers, sections of virgin forest at the heads of Porters Creek and Ramsey Prong, and the magnificent views from Mt. LeConte.

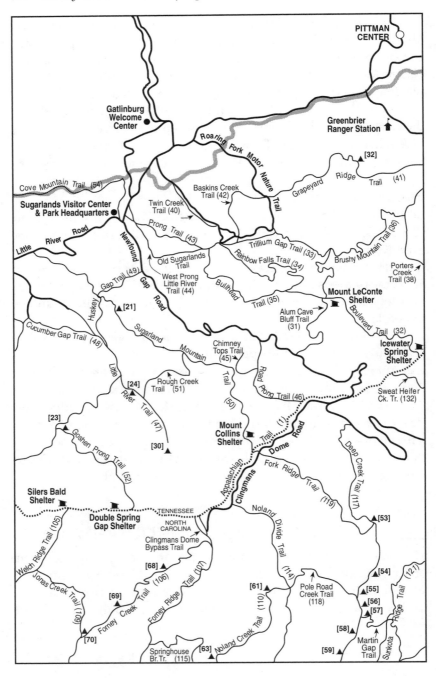

Mt. LeConte (elevation 6,593 feet) is a magnificent solitary peak, 5 miles by trail from the A.T. and main ridge. The northern side of Mt. LeConte is the highest base-to-summit hike in the East, rising about 5,000 feet in a distance of less than 5 miles.

Roaring Fork Motor Nature Trail is a self-guided, paved drive along the base of Mt. LeConte that is closed to RV's and closed in winter. You can purchase an information brochure at the beginning of this road that is keyed to numbered natural history and historical points. The Motor Nature Trail follows the beautiful Roaring Fork past a cliff face called "A Thousand Drips." This weeping water-seep is especially beautiful when frozen.

The Greenbrier Area can be reached from Gatlinburg by heading east on US 321. Mt. LeConte is accessible by trails beginning either from Newfound Gap Road or Cherokee Orchard Road. Access to the Greenbrier Cove Area is by way of Greenbrier Cove Road, a narrow gravel road that follows the Little Pigeon River to Greenbrier Ranger Station before forking into two deadend roads. There are no Park campgrounds in the area, but there are numerous private campgrounds nearby, especially along US 321.

Trail Descriptions

Five trails ascend Mt. LeConte. Two trails are accessible from Newfound Gap Road: Alum Cave Bluff Trail (31) and Boulevard Trail (32). The other three trails start from Cherokee Orchard Road: Trillium Gap Trail (33), Rainbow Falls Trail (34), and Bullhead Trail (35).

Lowland trails in the Greenbrier Area are less strenuous than those to the top of Mt. LeConte. These trail include Ramsey Cascade Trail (37), Porters Creek Trail (38), Old Settlers Trail (39), Twin Creeks Road Trail (40), Grapeyard Ridge Trail (41), and Baskins Creek Trail (42). Two connector trails join the horse stables at Sugarlands with the Cherokee Orchard Area: Prong Trail (43) and West Prong Little River Trail (44).

Alum Cave Bluff Trail (31)

This strenuous trail climbs nearly 2,600 feet in 5 miles from the trailhead to the main ridge of Mt. LeConte. In my opinion, it is the most beautiful trail to Mt. LeConte. There are numerous fantastic overlooks of the main ridge and the West Prong of the Little Pigeon

River Valley. This trail is also the shortest route up LeConte. If you can only hike one trail in the Park, do this one!

The trailhead is between two parking areas on Newfound Gap Road about 4 miles below Newfound Gap. The first mile of this trail is fairly level and travels through a lush, beautiful forest beside a stream. The trail then gradually climbs to several lookouts from side ridges before reaching Alum Cave Bluff. The "cave" is actually a 200-yard long overhanging bluff. Most day hikers stop here before returning to the trailhead.

Beyond Alum Cave Bluff, the trail begins a steeper incline around the mountain and uses switchbacks up through evergreen forest towards the summit. Near the summit, there are sections of cable hand-holds through an area that is often covered in ice during the winter and early spring.

Upon reaching the broad, relatively flat summit of Mt. LeConte, there are incredible views back toward the western half of the Smokies from the "Clifftops." I consider the views from this over-look to be among the best in the Smokies.

Boulevard Trail (32)

This moderate trail is accessible from the A.T., 2.7 miles east of Newfound Gap. It gradually ascends a narrow connecting ridge and reaches the eastern end of Mt. LeConte. This high ridge trail is one of the easier routes to the summit because of its higher elevation trailhead (elevation 5,000 feet).

There is one major gap along the Boulevard Trail where the trail drops approximately 500 feet prior to regaining this elevation. From the gap, the trail follows along a magnificent, knife-edge ridge with incredible views of the Greenbrier Valley thousands of feet below! The trail circles around the end of the main ridge where several landslides have removed short sections of the trail.

From the northeastern end of Mt. LeConte, a short side trail leads to Myrtle Point, an overlook with incredible views along the eastern ridge. This is the best spot for watching the sunrise, but the view has been clouded-in two out of the three times I have been there at dawn.

Trillium Gap Trail (33)

This mostly strenuous trail travels a total of 8.9 miles. For the first 2.5

Mt. LeConte-Greenbrier Backcountry Campsites

Campsite	Number	Elevation	Use	Hikers	Horses
Porters Flat	31	3400	Medium	15	No
Injun Creek	32	2280	Medium	8	No
Settlers Camp	33	1960	Medium	12	No
Mt. LeConte Shelter		6440	Rationed	12	No
LeConte Lodge			Private		Yes
			Reservation Required		

miles, the trail follows an easy path around the lower slope of Mt. LeConte to Grotto Falls. The trail becomes strenuous after Grotto Falls, climbing 3,300 feet to the summit of Mt. LeConte in 5.5 miles.

The first part of Trillium Gap Trail leads easily through huge hemlock trees to Grotto Falls, a small overhanging cascade where you can walk behind the 30-foot veil of water. The hike to the falls is an easy walk that I recommend to anyone who cannot physically hike the more difficult trails in the Park.

After the falls, the trail begins a more strenuous ascent to Trillium Gap. At the gap, the trail joins Brushy Mountain Trail (36), which continues another .5 miles to the open summit of Brushy Mountain. The climb up Mt. LeConte becomes more strenuous after the gap as it steadily ascends the north face of the mountain on a series of long switchbacks.

The upper half of Trillium Gap Trail is especially beautiful, passing through a variety of forest types. In the spring, you can find late-blooming flowers at lower elevations when early-blooming species are still showing color at higher elevations. Because you gain 3,000 to 4,000 feet in elevation along this trail, you can observe different flowers in a single day that are normally seen blooming over a period of a month to six weeks.

Near the summit, the trail wraps around the northern side of Mt. LeConte passing through an area where every piece of ground seems to be covered by ferns and mosses. *Note:* I recommend taking the trail from the parking area for Grotto Falls Trail at the beginning of Roaring Fork Motor Nature Trail.

Rainbow Falls Trail (34)

This strenuous creek headwater trail climbs 3,800 feet in 6 miles to the summit of Mt. LeConte. The trailhead is at Cherokee Orchard Parking Area.

The trail leads steadily uphill for about 1.75 miles to Rainbow Falls. Rainbow Falls is normally a narrow cascade varying in size with rainfall; I have only seen it during dry periods when it was not very impressive. The walk to this waterfall is longer and much more strenuous than the hike to Grotto Falls.

From the waterfall to the summit, the trail becomes more strenuous, climbing steadily along a very rocky trail with only a few good lookouts. For this reason, Rainbow Falls Trail is my least favorite route to the summit.

Bullhead Trail (35)

This strenuous high ridge trail is a more gradual route to the summit of Mt. LeConte. It gains 3,800 feet in 6 miles. While this trail is the longest hike to the summit, it is highly recommended. The trailhead is at Cherokee Orchard Parking Area.

Along its lower half, the trail winds below impressive rock outcrops. Then it gradually climbs to reach a side ridge that leads steadily to the summit.

Brushy Mountain Trail (36)

This strenuous creek headwater trail leads from Greenbrier Cove towards Mt. LeConte. The nearly 5-mile climb gains just over 3,000 feet in elevation.

The trail is especially beautiful as it gradually climbs the backside of Brushy Mountain to reach a side ridge at Trillium Gap. The trail continues north from the gap for about .5 miles to the open heath bald on the summit, with impressive views of Mt. LeConte.

Ramsey Cascade Trail (37)

This moderate, 4-mile trail begins at the end of the left fork of the narrow gravel road into Greenbrier Cove. This lower creek trail is very popular because it leads through a dazzling section of virgin forest with huge trees, giant boulders, and massive rock slides. This is an ideal trail to experience old growth forest.

The flow down Ramsey Cascades varies greatly with rainfall but is especially spectacular after thunderstorms. The stream is surrounded by slippery rocks, so use great care and do not climb on the rocks. Several hikers have been killed while attempting to climb on wet rocks around the cascade.

Porters Creek Trail (38)

This strenuous lower creek trail leads through magnificent forest for nearly 3 miles to Porters Flat Campsite #31. The trail is noted for the variety of spring wildflowers in late April and early May.

The trail is very easy for the first 2 miles. It leads past the area called Porters Flats, an unusually large, flat area at the base of Mt. LeConte. The flats were obviously used as farm fields. The forest has regrown with a very open understory and the area is full of old rock walls (off the trail) that more curious hikers can explore.

Beyond the Flats, the trail crosses Porters Creek on a bridge and continues through several groves of magnificent hemlock and poplar trees before it deadends at Porters Flat Campsite #31. This beautiful camp has numerous sites nestled next to the creek and surrounded by huge trunks from fallen trees.

A rough man-way continues past the campsite and scrambles up to the A.T. near Charlies Bunion. This trail is not recommended because it is nearly impassible, apparently kept worn only by "sliding" hikers.

Old Settlers Trail (39)

This moderate, nearly 16-mile trail creates a loop between the A.T., Mt. Leconte, and the Greenbrier and Cosby Areas. The trail is too long for a reasonable day hike, but you could hike parts of the pretty eastern end of the trail near Albright Grove.

This lowland trail mostly follows along roadbeds past numerous old farm sites and the most impressive rock walls in the Park. The trail tends to ramble in and out of two major side coves, which forces unnecessary elevation climbs but adds variety to the trail.

Twin Creeks Road Trail (40)

This strenuous lowland trail climbs 800 feet in 1.8 miles. The trail is perfect for day hiking and is especially rich in spring wildflowers.

There are also a great variety of summer and fall flowers. Because the trail follows between LeConte Creek and Cherokee Orchard Road, you are never far from road noises.

Grapeyard Ridge Trail (41)
This relatively easy trail leads 7.5 miles across the lowlands to connect Greenbrier with Roaring Fork Motor Nature Trail. The trail goes on old roads, by old farms, and along low ridges with only moderate ups and downs. There are very few lookouts of Mt. LeConte in the summer, but this is a nice trail for viewing spring and summer wildflowers.

Baskins Creek Trail (42)
This easy, nearly 2.7-mile trail links Grapeyard Ridge Trail (41) to Trillium Gap Trail (33) near Cherokee Orchard. The trail is primarily recommended as part of a loop from Greenbrier to Cherokee Orchard Area, but it would also make an enjoyable wildflower walk. *Note:* The eastern trailhead is along the one-way Roaring Fork Motor Nature Trail, so you may want to hike just part of the trail to avoid the need for a car shuttle.

Prong Trail (43)
This moderate lowland trail gains 1,000 feet in 2.5 miles. It travels from the stables near Sugarlands Visitor Center to trailheads in the Cherokee Orchard Area. Parts of the trail are extremely muddy and deeply mired. This trail is best enjoyed on horseback.

West Prong Little River Trail (44)
This moderate trail climbs to trailheads at Cherokee Orchard along a 3-mile lowland route. Like Prong Trail (43), this trail is best enjoyed on horseback. I would recommend this trail over Prong Trail for hikers who want the more enjoyable route connecting Sugarlands with the base of Mt. LeConte.

Recommended Hiking
The best day hikes in the area are Alum Cave Bluff Trail (31), the first part of Trillium Gap Trail (33), Ramsey Cascades Trail (37), and

Porters Creek Trail (38).

There are several multi-day loops around Mt. LeConte. A highly recommended 4-day trip starts at Cherokee Orchard, follows along the lower mountains to Greenbrier Cove, and then climbs Mt. LeConte (use trail 42, 41, 36, and 33). One of several trails (trail 34 or 35) can be hiked to return to Cherokee Orchard.

I also highly recommend a loop that starts at Roaring Fork Parking Area and goes to Grotto Falls on Trillium Gap Trail (33). From the gap, ascend to the summit of Mt. LeConte and return by way of Bullhead Trail (35).

_____ Elkmont-Tremont Areas

The Elkmont and Tremont Areas are linked by the scenic Little River Road (TN 73), which connects Sugarlands to the Tremont Area along the northern slopes of the Park. These valleys and most of the boundary ridges were extensively logged, but there are still pockets of virgin forest. Prime area attractions include virgin forest above Laurel Falls, numerous connector trails that allow many loop possibilities, and lovely, lowland trails past old farms.

The lower end of Elkmont Valley is heavily developed. The old Wonderland Hotel and private vacation homes that were not removed when the Park was established can be seen near the campground. These have now been vacated but the fate of the structures has not been determined. The Tremont Watershed is the next major valley west of Elkmont and its streams roughly parallel Elkmont's drainage system.

Elkmont-Tremont Areas are easily reached from deadend side roads off of Little River Road, which runs through the Park connecting Gatlinburg and Townsend, Tennessee. Elkmont Road leads to Elkmont Campground and Ranger Station and then forks into two roads which soon deadend. Tremont Road follows the Middle Prong River to Tremont Ranger Station and the Great Smoky Mountain Institute at Tremont. The road becomes gravel and deadends about 4 miles further up the valley.

Elkmont Campground is the largest and most popular in the Park and is almost always full. This campground almost certainly

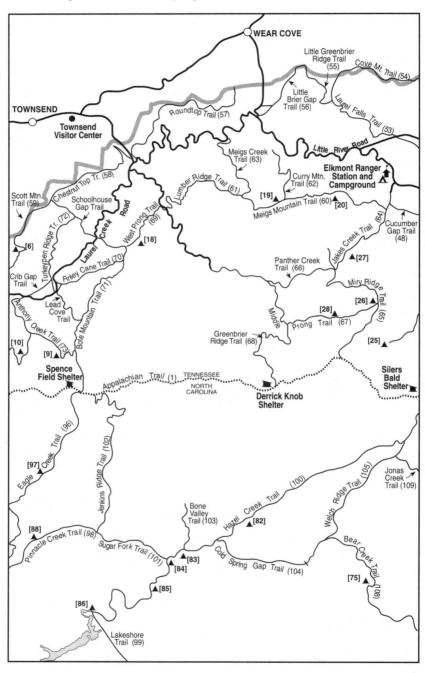

requires advanced reservations. There are numerous private camp-grounds in and around Gatlinburg and Townsend that are close to Elkmont-Tremont Areas.

There are no camping facilities along the road into Tremont, although there is an environmental education camp, the Great Smoky Mountain Institute at Tremont. This Institute is run by the Smoky Mountain Natural History Association and provides school and summer programs, and weekend workshops. For more information, contact the GSMNHA (see Appendix C).

Trail Descriptions

From Elkmont and Tremont Valleys, there are six major trails that ascend and connect with the A.T. along the main ridge. These trails allow numerous backpacking loops.

Along the northern border of the Park, several trails were at one time grouped together as the "Boundary Trails." These trails followed the Park boundary along low ridges from Sugarlands to the summit of Cove Mountain and to the northwestern end of the Park at Ace Gap near Abrams Creek. They are more suitable for day hiking because there are no campsites along most of them.

Chimney Top Trail and Road Prong Trail are somewhat isolated from the other trails in the area, but these two are included in this section because road access to them is from Newfound Gap Road near the trailhead to Alum Cave Bluff.

Meigs Mountain Trail (60) and Lumber Ridge Trail (61) together link Elkmont and Tremont Valleys along lowland ridges. The trails generally follow old roads and parts of old railroad grades through second growth forest. Along these trails, there are many uniformed-sized tulip poplar and black locust trees. Uniform-sized trees result when old fields and clearings revert to forest.

Two short connector trails, Curry Mountain Trail (62) and Meigs Creek Trail (63), serve to connect Meigs Mountain with trailheads along the paved Little River Road.

Two additional trails connect Elkmont and Tremont along the middle slopes over the side ridge that separate these two watersheds: Jakes Creek Trail (64) and Miry Ridge Trail (65). Two side trails connect Miry Ridge Trail with trails in the Tremont Valley: Panther Creek Trail (66) and the upper end of Middle Prong Trail (67).

Chimney Tops Trail (45)

This trail is the steepest per mile listed in this book. In its middle section, the trail is extremely strenuous, climbing over 1,300 feet to a side ridge in a little over 1 mile. However, the trail is a very popular 2-mile loop.

The Chimney Tops, a series of vertical "chimney-like" rock that towers 50 feet above the picnic area, affords incredible views. The view from the base of the first outcrop is nearly as good as those on the higher, more dangerous "Tops". These outcrops are composed of crumbly Anakeesta sandstone, so use great care while climbing.

Note: There is an overgrown, nearly impassible man-way connector from the Chimneys to Sugarland Mountain, but it is nearly impassible with a pack.

Road Prong Trail (46)

This extremely strenuous creek headwater trail gains nearly 2,000 feet in 2.5 miles. The trail climbs from Chimney Top Trail to the A.T. following the old roadway of the first commercial wagon road.

This exhausting and very rugged trail has at least one dangerous creek crossing near its lower trailhead. And, the route can be confusing near its upper end because it literally travels through the middle of the stream for a short section.

Little River Trail (47)

This moderate lower creek trail rises 1,400 feet in 5 miles. It allows access to almost every trail in Elkmont Valley. The lower end of the trail is gradual and ideal for day hikes because it follows Little River upstream. After the intersection with Goshen Prong Trail (52), the trail continues along a smaller gravel jeep road to deadend at the pleasant Three Forks Campsite #30.

Cucumber Gap Trail (48)

This delightful trail makes a nice day hike from the end of the road near Elkmont Campground. It connects Little River Trail (47) to Meigs Mountain Trail (60) and Jakes Creek Trail (64). The trail is an easy hike, only climbing 300 feet in 2.3 miles through a relatively low

Elkmont-Tremont Backcountry Campsites

Campsite	Number	Elevation	Use	Hikers	Horses
West Prong	18	1600	Medium	8	No
Upper Henderson	19	2880	Light	8	8
Henderson King	20	2520	Medium	10	10
Medicine Branch	21	3780	Medium	8	8
Camp Rock	23	3200	Rationed	8	No
Rough Creek	24	2860	Rationed	14	14
Lower Buckeye Gap	25	3540	Light	8	No
Dripping Spring	26	4400	Medium	8	8
Lower Jakes Gap	27	3520	Medium	8	8
Marks Cove	28	3490	Medium	20	20
Three Forks	30	3400	Medium	12	No

gap. The trees that shade this trail are good examples of re-growth following the end of logging in the early 1930s. The extremely large leaves of the cucumber magnolia (up to two feet long) are especially noticeable near the gap.

Huskey Gap Trail (49)

About .75 miles south from the trail intersection of Cucumber Gap Trail (48) and Little River Trail (47), this trail gives lateral access to Sugarlands Mountain Trail (50) and continues over the ridge and down to Newfound Gap Road, nearly 2 miles from Sugarlands Visitor Center.

The trailhead along Newfound Gap Road is hard to find, but it is about 1.7 miles from the Little River Road intersection at Sugarlands. From this trailhead, the trail climbs strenuously to a ridge through second growth forest, a gain of 1,200 feet in 2 miles. The trail to the ridge from Little River Trail only requires a 500-foot elevation gain.

Sugarland Mountain Trail (50)

This trail follows the entire ridge of Sugarland Mountain from Little River Road at Fighting Creek Gap to the A.T. near Mt. Collins Shelter. This long but moderate high ridge trail climbs 3,700 feet in over 12 miles. There are a half-dozen spectacular lookouts from the ridge to the valleys below, most of which are northwest of Huskey Gap.

The trail climbs steeply at first out of Fighting Creek Gap to the lower end of the ridge but then remains a relatively gradual climb for about 6 miles. The trail is unusually pleasant above Huskey Gap Trail, winding in and out of small coves to Medicine Branch Bluff Campsite #21. This is the only campsite along Sugarland Mountain. It is a lovely campsite, nestled among huge boulders. The piped spring at the campsite is the most dependable water source along the ridge.

The uppermost part of the trail passes through a dark, evergreen forest prior to reaching Mt. Collins Shelter. The spruce and fir trees around the shelter have declined in recent years, but the ground is still lush and green with tree seedlings, ferns, and mosses.

Rough Creek Trail (51)

This strenuous creek headwater trail laterally connects the upper third of Little River Trail (47) with Sugarland Mountain Trail (50). It climbs steadily for about 3 miles, following above the creek along an old jeep road. From the trail, there are a couple of good views of Mt. Collins and the main ridge.

Goshen Prong Trail (52)

This strenuous, 7.3-mile trail connects Elkmont Valley with the A.T. The lower 3 miles, a very easy and enjoyable hike, follows along Goshen Prong. The trail becomes more strenuous just after the intersection with a spur trail, which leads .75 miles to Lower Buckeye Campsite #25. Rising about 2,500 feet in 4.5 miles, the trail climbs steadily to the headwaters of Goshen Prong and intersects the A.T. about .5 miles from Double Springs Shelter.

Three Forks Campsite #30 and Lower Buckeye Campsite #25 are highly recommended. They are somewhat isolated because both sites are at the ends of spur trails off the main connector trails, but both are easily reached from Elkmont and are ideal for a moderate, introductory overnighter.

Laurel Falls Trail (53)

This trail leads from the lower end of Sugarland Mountain Trail at Fighting Creek Gap to Laurel Falls and the firetower on Cove Mountain. The trail is rated strenuous because it climbs nearly 1,800 feet in 4 miles along a side ridge to the ridge of Cove Mountain.

The first 1.3 miles are only moderate in difficulty. Due to heavy use, it is paved to prevent erosion. Baby strollers can be used on this trail as far as the falls. Most people only hike this far, but there is a gorgeous section of virgin forest about .5 miles beyond the falls. For about .5 miles, the trail passes trees with four- and five-foot diameters.

The trail continues through thick forest to the summit of Cove Mountain where there are now only limited views through the trees. Formerly, you could climb Cove Mountain Firetower for incredible views, but installation of equipment on the firetower in 1992 prevents access.

Cove Mountain Trail (54)

This moderate low ridge trail is the most eastern of the boundary trails. The trail follows a gradual jeep road for 9 miles from Park Headquarters at Sugarlands to Cove Mountain Firetower. There are few views from this trail except in the winter.

Near the trailhead at Sugarlands, the trail passes the wheelchair-accessible Cataract Falls. Beyond the falls, the trail rises more steeply and climbs past several small waterfalls before crossing a stream (last water!) and reaching the ridge. Then the trail gradually follows the side of the ridge up to the tower.

Little Brier Ridge Trail (55)

This strenuous trail connects Cove Mountain with the Little Greenbrier Area. It wraps around Cove Mountain and along a low connecting ridge for over 4 miles. There are a few views into the surrounding valleys and southwest towards Cades Cove. There are no dependable water sources along this trail.

Little Brier Branch Road Trail (56)

This old road (gated and not open to traffic) gradually descends 2 miles from Little Brier Gap into the Little Greenbrier Area. *Note:* Park maps are in error because they indicate that this trail is only 1 mile long when it is actually 1 mile above and below the school-house. One of the few dependable water sources on the boundary trails is a few hundred yards down this trail from the gap.

The homestead of the Walker Sisters, five old maids that lived self-sufficiently following the death of their father, is located .5 miles from the gap. Several of the original home and farm buildings have been restored. This homestead makes an interesting historical destination for a easy day hike out of Metcalf Bottoms Picnic Area.

The Little Greenbrier Schoolhouse, an interesting restored school-house and church, is located about 1 mile from Metcalf Bottoms Picnic Area on a short side road. A popular place to visit, the one-room school contains chestnut timbers over 24 inches in diameter.

Roundtop Trail (57)

This trail follows old logging roads from the western end of Little Brier Ridge Trail (55) to the Little River at the Townsend "Y," the intersection of the Little River and Laurel Creeks (sometimes spelled Townsend "Wye"). This low ridge trail is known as an excellent wildflower trail in the spring.

There is no bridge across the Little River at the western trailhead, and the trailhead is not marked here but can be found by wading across the river immediately above the junction of the two rivers. The crossing is knee deep during low water and swimmers have created a low, submerged-rock dam just beyond the upper edge of the field at the "Y". Do not attempt to cross following heavy rains. I recommend hiking this trail from west to east in case there are afternoon thunderstorms, which could make the river crossing impassable!

Chestnut Top Trail (58)

This 4-mile, moderate trail continues west along the Park boundary towards Cades Cove, following low ridges on an old jeep road. The trail is especially noted for its display of spring wildflowers. It is recommended over Roundtop Trail (57) because it does not have any major stream crossings.

The trail rises steadily from the parking area of the Townsend "Y" before reaching and rounding a low ridge. The trail then becomes more gradual as it travels to the trailhead at Schoolhouse Gap and the eastern trailhead of Scott Mountain Trail (59).

The only dependable water in this section is below Schoolhouse Gap, a few hundred yards west of the gravel jeep road. At the gap, you have to drop down along the route of the original overgrown Bote Mountain Road for about 100 yards to the nearest water in a rhododendron thicket.

Scott Mountain Trail (59)
This trail continues west from Schoolhouse Gap. It is further described in the section on Cades Cove.

Meigs Mountain Trail (60)
This moderate lowland trail climbs 1,100 feet in 6 miles. It is a pleasant and very gradual trail that rises along the lower slope of Meigs Mountain. The trail begins near Elkmont Campground at the intersection of Cucumber Gap Trail (48) and Jakes Creek Trail (64).

There are two campsites along the trail. King Branch Campsite #20 is very lovely with a lot of sites. Upper Henderson Campsite #19 is in a dark stand of black locust and has few level sites.

Lumber Ridge Trail (61)
This moderate, 4-mile lowland trail links Tremont and Meigs Mountain Trail (60) to Elkmont. The western end of the trail rises steeply from the Great Smoky Mountain Institute at Tremont, but the rest of this trail is relatively easy with only moderate elevation changes. There is no dependable water along this trail.

Curry Mountain Trail (62)
This trail begins a few hundred feet east of Metcalf Bottoms Picnic Area at a gated trailhead (best to park at the picnic area). It gradually climbs and circles a dry side ridge with no water sources. Following the ridge on an old road, the trail reaches a family cemetery at the intersection with Meigs Mountain Trail. Horseflies can be exceptionally annoying in mid-summer.

Meigs Creek Trail (63)

This moderate creek headwater trail climbs 1,100 feet in 6 miles. The trailhead is beside the parking area on Little River Road at the Sinks, a well-known water cascade and swimming area. *Note:* The trailhead begins west of the parking area behind a trail sign, not along the deadend trail to the left.

The trail ascends steadily up and around a low ridge and climbs into the lush valley of Meigs Creek. The trail then gradually ascends beside Meigs Creek nearly to the ridge.

This trail is much prettier than Curry Mountain Trail (62), but it requires over a dozen stream crossings and is not recommended after heavy rains. This is a superb trail for day hiking. Some particularly beautiful stands of trees can be found along the upper half of this trail.

Combine this trail and Curry Mountain Trail for an 8.5-mile day hike. You will have to leave cars at both trailheads (the Sinks and Metcalf Bottoms) along Little River Road.

Jakes Creek Trail (64)

This creek headwater trail follows along an old jeep road for nearly 3 miles from Elkmont Valley to Jakes Gap. The lower end is strenuous, rising over 1,500 feet. From the gap, the trail continues about 1 mile, with a 500-foot elevation gain, to the summit of Blanket Mountain. There are limited views in the summer from rocks near the site of a former firetower. Panther Creek Trail (66) connects Jakes Gap with the Middle Prong Trail (67) in Tremont Valley.

Miry Ridge Trail (65)

This moderate ridge trail links Jakes Gap with the A.T. The trail climbs 900 in 5 miles as it follows along Dripping Springs Mountain. Numerous springs normally flow from fractures in rock outcrops along the trail.

When I hiked this trail during an unusually dry year, there was no water to be found except far below Dripping Spring Mountain Campsite #29, a very small campsite, hardly more than a grassy area beside the trail. Beyond the campsite, the trail steeply ascends the encircling ridge to Cold Spring Knob and the A.T.

Panther Creek Trail (66)

This strenuous creek headwater trail rises nearly 1,500 feet in 2 miles as it travels from Middle Prong Trail to Jakes Gap. The trail descends steadily down a side ridge and follows along a stream for its last mile before the intersection with the lower half of Middle Prong Trail.

Middle Prong Trail (67)

Upstream from the Great Smoky Mountain Institute at Tremont, the road becomes gravel for 3 miles where it is gated at a river crossing near the site of former logging camps. This trail begins at the gate.

It is a moderate lower creek trail that rises about 1,500 feet in 4 miles. About .5 miles from the trailhead, there is a beautiful cascading waterfall, which would be a nice destination for an easy day hike.

The trail continues on a wide railroad grade up the valley. The old railroad grade actually has four switchbacks up one steep section before it intersects Greenbrier Ridge Trail (68). The Middle Prong Trail turns abruptly from the main valley and gradually ascends along railroad grade up the side valley to Marks Cove Campsite #28. From this nice campsite, the trail narrows as it gradually climbs through open forest to Miry Ridge.

Greenbrier Ridge Trail (68)

This moderate low ridge trail begins at the upper end of Middle Prong Trail (67). It climbs 1,300 feet in 4 miles along the old railroad grade. The trail leaves the main valley, makes a major turn to travel through pleasant forest, and circles up and around a side ridge along a gradual grade to the main ridge at Derricks Knob.

West Prong Trail (69)

This trail serves as a major connector from Tremont Valley to the Cades Cove Area. It is a moderate lowland trail that passes through lovely second growth forest. The trail only gains 650 over nearly 3 miles, winding gradually along slopes and passing by several old homesites.

West Prong Campsite (#18) is one of my favorite in the area, even though it appears to be heavily used. The campsite is by a fast-flowing stream and there are numerous tent sites. Foxfire, a bioluminescent fungus, is unusually abundant here in mid-summer.

Finley Cane Trail (70)

Near West Prong Campsite #18, this trail intersects Bote Mountain Trail (71). This lowland trail connects Laurel Creek Road and trails to Cades Cove. This moderate, 3-mile trail has an elevation change of only 650 feet. It is an ideal trail for a day hike because of the various ferns and wildflowers and the easy access from Laurel Creek Road.

Bote Mountain Road Trail (71)

Near West Prong Campsite #18, this trail intersects Finley Cane Trail (70). This strenuous low ridge trail gains over 3,000 feet in 6 miles from Laurel Creek Road to the A.T. at Spence Field.

The original wagon road was completed in the mid-1830s from Tuckaleechee Cove to end at the main ridge because money could not be raised to continue the road into North Carolina. Parts of the original road (Schoolhouse Gap Trail) can be used to connect to Laurel Creek Road and beyond to Whiteoak Sink and Schoolhouse Gap.

The northern section of this trail has no water sources, but it is well-graded and gradual to the junction with Anthony Creek Trail (73). From this intersection, the trail becomes more narrow, rockier, and deeply eroded. The last 1.7 miles to the main ridge is especially beautiful. The thick evergreen rhododendrons forms a tunnel around and over the road. There are several water sources between Anthony Creek Trail (73) and the A.T.

Turkeypen Ridge Trail (72)

This relatively easy lowland trail rises over a low ridge and serves as a pretty, 3.6-mile connector trail towards Laurel Creek Road and Cave Cove. Along the trail you will have enclosed views of several small forest coves and seasonal wildflower displays. This is a pleasant trail for day hiking. It intersects with Crib Gap Trail, a short, lowland connector trail to Cades Cove It is heavily used by horses.

Recommended Hiking

Highly recommended day hikes in the area include Cucumber Gap Trail (48), Laurel Falls Trail (53), Chestnut Top Trail (58), Meigs Creek Trail (63), and Turkey Pen Gap Trail (72).

There are innumerable possibilities for backpacking loops around and between these valleys. A great 4-night, 32-mile loop out of

Elkmont follows Jakes Creek Trail (64), winds along Miry Ridge Trail (65) to the A.T., and then runs along the ridge to Goshen Prong Trail (52). Return to Elkmont along Little River Trail (47) and Cucumber Gap Trail (48). Use campsite #25 and #30.

_ Cades Cove-Abrams Creek Areas

Cades Cove (approximate elevation 1,800 feet) is one of the most visited and most unique areas of the Park. Major features of this area include abundant wildlife, great bicycling, interesting geology, prime fishing spots, and the most extensive collection of historical structures in the Park.

Cades Cove is probably the best place in the Park for viewing wildlife. Because of its large uninterrupted forest area and relative isolation from Tennessee towns, there are great concentrations of wildlife, especially deer, bear, and boar. This area is so full of wildlife that I can nearly guarantee that you will see deer, and an occasional skunk or wild turkey.

At dawn or dusk, be sure to drive the 11-mile Cades Cove Loop Road, which circles through grassy meadows. On my last visit, I saw one of the reintroduced, radio-collared red wolves crossing a field beside the Loop Road. This road is notorious for "bear-jams" and "bambi-jams," which is when people stop their cars to take pictures of wildlife and traffic backs up.

Cades Cove has a bicycle rental shop, which opens at 9:00 AM. It is best to bring your own bike so that you can ride early in the morning or late in the afternoon, which is when you are most likely to see wildlife. The Loop Road is gated to motor traffic until 10:00 A.M. on summer Saturdays exclusively for use by bicyclists, and there are two cross-valley access roads that offer shorter biking loops.

The grassy, open meadow and nearly level valley floor of Cades Cove is actually a "window" exposing the geologically younger underlying limestone. During the period when continental plates pushed together and formed the high Appalachian ridges, massive forces uplifted older rocks thousands of feet and moved them westward to overlay the younger sedimentary rocks formed from ancient inland seas.

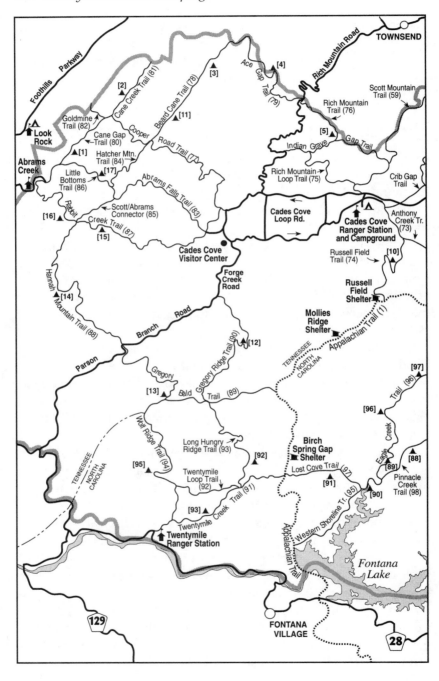

Areas of older rocks have eroded away to expose sections of younger limestone and create the unique soils, sinkholes, and caves in present-day Cades Cove. All Park caves have recently been closed to exploration because of high levels of radon gas and in order to protect endangered cave animals.

Cades Cove is underlain with limestone bedrock and supports plants that are only commonly found on limestone derived soils. This soil type promotes abundant aquatic plant food for fish. Abrams Creek is considered by many to be the best fishing area in the entire Park.

Cades Cove is rich in pioneer history. There is an excellent museum (open seasonally), an operating water mill, and numerous reconstructed pioneer farms and churches. Along Cades Cove Loop Road, you will find numerous historical exhibits, as well as abundant roadside spots for picnics.

Cades Cove-Abrams Creek Areas are located at the western end of the Park. Cades Cove is usually reached from Laurel Creek Road, which joins Little River Road near Townsend. Cades Cove Loop Road begins at Cades Cove Campground and Ranger Station and allows easy access to area trails.

Abrams Creek Area, which includes a ranger station and primitive campground, is best approached from US 129 near the intersection of the Foothills Parkway south of Maryville, Tennessee. From Chilhowee Lake, follow signs into Happy Valley to the end of the road at Abrams Creek Campground. Watch carefully for signs along Happy Valley Road because there are several obscure turns. Happy Valley Road can also be reached from Murray Gap near the Look Rock Observation Tower.

Laurel Creek Road is the only road open year round linking Cades Cove with Little River Road (TN 73) and nearby Townsend. Two one-way gravel roads, Rich Mountain Road and Parsons Branch Road (both closed in winter), lead out of Cades Cove. These primitive roads are only open from late April through November.

Rich Mountain Road provides a one-way exit to Tuckaleechee Cove and Townsend just north of the Cove. The road becomes two-way at the Park boundary and allows easy access to Ace Gap Trail (79) and Rich Mountain Trail (76). Parsons Branch Road is a one-way exit towards the southwest end of the Park at Calderwood Lake.

Cades Cove-Abrams Creek-Rich Mountain Backcountry Campsites

Campsite	Number	Elevation	Use	Hikers	Horses
Cooper Road	1	1200	Light	10	10
Cane Creek	2	1320	Light	10	No
Hesse Creek	3	1360	Light	10	10
Kelly Gap	4	1930	Light	10	10
Rich Mountain	5	3460	Rationed	8	8
Turkeypen Ridge	6	3400	Medium	10	No
Ace Gap	7	1680	Light	10	10
Anthony Creek	9	3200	Medium	6	6
Ledbetter Ridge	10	3000	Rationed	8	8
Beard Cane	11	1530	Light	10	6
Forge Creek	12	2600	Medium	8	No
Sheep Pen Gap	13	4640	Medium	12	12
Flint Gap	14	2050	Light	8	8
Rabbit Creek	15	1550	Medium	8	8
Scotts Gap	16	1760	Rationed	8	8
Little Bottoms	17	1240	Medium	10	No

While Parsons Branch Road is a very charming drive, it is a slow road to travel (but why hurry?).

Cades Cove Campground (121 sites) is located at the beginning of the 11-mile Cades Cove Loop Road. The campground is usually full except in winter. There are problems with skunk and ravens at the campground, so keep food inside your car and trash in animal-proof cans. A small general store (the only one in the Park) at the campground has snacks and ice cream.

Abrams Creek Primitive Campground is along the western end of the Park. The campground only has 20 sites and is heavily used on weekends. The smaller campgrounds, like Abrams Creek, are my favorite in the Park because they are usually quieter and seem more "relaxed." One part of the creek beside the campground is deep enough for swimming.

Trail Descriptions

There is an especially beautiful nature trail that loops around a low ridge behind the campground. This short trail follows a small creek up a pleasant, narrow valley before rising to a low ridge. There is a beautiful view through a small opening in the leaves across the meadow towards Rich Mountain.

Several trails lead to the summit of Rich Mountain along the northern border of the Park that allow connections with other area trails: Rich Mountain Loop Trail (75) and Rich Mountain Trail (76).

All the lowland trails north of the main ridge have a special charm quite different from those along the higher elevations or southern slopes.

Anthony Creek Trail (73)

This strenuous creek headwater trail begins at Cades Cove Picnic Area, climbs to the lateral ridge of Bote Mountain, and accesses the grassy Spence Field. Following wide footpaths through an especially beautiful forest, the trail climbs 1,800 in 3.5 miles and is ideal for day hikes. Anthony Creek Campsite #9 is located in a beautiful section of forest.

Russell Field Trail (74)

This strenuous, mostly high ridge trail leads from the middle of Anthony Creek Trail to Russell Field Shelter on the main ridge. It climbs nearly 1,900 feet in 3.5 miles and travels through sections of beautiful cove hardwood forest. The only water is at the upper end of the trail. The middle section is surprisingly level. While Russell Field, for the most part, is overgrown, there are some great views from the A.T. when traveling east to Spence Field.

Rich Mountain Loop Trail (75)

This moderate trail is a rewarding day hike to the ridge summit of Rich Mountain where there are a few great lookouts over Cades Cove Valley. The trail climbs 1,700 feet in 7.5 miles.

The western half of this loop, which is rocky in places and heavily used by horses, follows jeep roads to the summit. There are few water sources after the lower creeks. The eastern half of this loop climbs steeply on switchbacks to a side ridge and then along a deeply-eroded trail. There is one great view of Cades Cove just prior to the intersection with Scott Mountain Trail (59).

Rich Mountain Trail (76)

From the Park boundary at Rich Mountain Road, this moderate high ridge trail climbs 1,500 feet in 4 miles. Almost all the elevation gain occurs in the western 2.3 miles to the summit of Rich Mountain, while the eastern 1.7 miles follows a nearly-level jeep road across the summit.

Rich Mountain Campsite #5 is located near the summit, just above a section of virgin forest. The water source for the shelter is about .3 miles away. The shelter was removed in 1995 and has a few level tent sites. There are a few good lookouts from the trail across the summit to the trailhead of Scott Mountain Trail (59).

Scott Mountain Trail (59)

This moderate, 3.6-mile trail is a combination of high ridges and low mountain slopes. It has a 1,600-foot elevation change. The trail could be used for a day hike out of Schoolhouse Gap or it could be included with part of Rich Mountain Loop Trail.

The trail begins at the eastern end of the nearly-level ridge of Rich Mountain and circles around the lush north side of Scott Mountain above a giant sink hole, Whiteoak Sink. The only dependable water source is at Turkey Pen Ridge Campsite #6, which is on the western end of the trail.

The trail continues to circle around the narrow ridge to Schoolhouse Gap and then on to Chestnut Top Trail (58). Along this narrow ridge connecting Scott Mountain and Schoolhouse Gap, you will find exposed sections of both Precambium and Ordovician rocks. Wildflowers and shrubs can be seen growing on the soils that developed from these distinctly different bedrock.

A gravel road leads from the intersection of Chestnut Top Trail to Turkeypen Ridge Trail (72) and then on to Laurel Creek Road. Adventurous hikers can follow old Bote Mountain Road (unmarked and unmaintained through this section but not too hard to follow) from Schoolhouse Gap into Whiteoak Sink Valley.

In the valley, there is a small waterfall that drops over a cliff and disappears into a sink hole. The man-way to this secret falls can be found beside a large tree marked with hatchet gashes about 50 feet north of where the road intersects Turkeypen Ridge Trail (72).

Whiteoak Sink Valley contained many old farms and is a great place for experienced hikers to explore off the trail. You can investigate old stone walls and find small sink holes and cave openings.

Cooper Road Trail (77)

This relatively easy, 10.5 mile lowland trail (gated road) connects Abrams Creek Area with Cades Cove, following the first wagon road that went into Cades Cove. There is only an 800-foot elevation change over 5.5 miles traveling west from Cades Cove Road to Hatcher Mountain Trail (84) then descends 1.7 miles to Cane Gap.

The trail rises from its western end through pleasant forest before reaching the low ridge and Beard Cane Creek Trail (78). There are several stream crossings and two low ridges to climb.

Beard Cane Trail (78)

This super easy creek headwater trail is located in the extreme northwest corner of the Park and follows an unusually flat valley with an average elevation change of 100 feet per mile. The 4-mile trail has two campsites: Beard Cane Campsite #11 and the more beautiful Hesse Creek Campsite #3. Both camping areas can be easily reached by trails from Abrams Creek Campground or Cades Cove Loop Road.

Ace Gap Trail (79)

From the northern trailhead of Beard Cane Trail, you can hike the Park boundary on this extremely easy trail that goes over to Rich Mountain Road. The trail only climbs 450 feet in 5.5 miles.

I have seen unusual sights along this trail at Kelley Gap Campsite

#4. One night a string of unblinking bioluminescent individual eyes floated head-high through the area. The sight was so exceptional that I got out of bed to investigate and found a type of firefly traveling one after another in a string. There must be all sorts of ghost stories because of this insect!

Cane Gap Trail (80)

This trail connects Abrams Creek Campground with Cane Creek Trail (81) and Cooper Road Trail (77) at Cane Gap. This creek headwater trail is rated moderate and climbs 500 feet gradually in 2.8 miles. The trail passes through some lovely forest and follows a pleasant stream for about 2 miles. This makes an excellent day hike from the campground. This trail route follows the original Cooper Road route to Cane Gap.

Cane Creek Trail (81)

This moderate lower creek trail leads 2 miles north of Cane Gap and Cooper Road Trails northeast from Abrams Creek Campground. The trail is primarily used by horses and for access to Cane Creek Campsite #2.

The northern trailhead begins on private property at the Park boundary, so this trail can really only be approached from the trailhead at Cane Gap. From Cane Gap, the trail descends steeply for about .5 miles before reaching the campsite at Cane Creek. The campsite is located in an area of small pines and scattered river cane that appears to have been burned by a forest fire in recent years. Expect raccoons in camp.

The trail continues along the creek with little elevation change to deadend at the Park boundary. The old boundary trail towards Ace Gap begins here, but it is not maintained and is obviously full of blowdowns.

Goldmine Trail (82)

This short but strenuous lowland trail starts from Cane Gap Trail (80). The nearly mile-long side trail climbs along an old roadway to deadend on private property at the western Park boundary. This historical area has unusual rock outcroppings and dug trenches. The trail is best explored as a day hike.

Abrams Falls Trail (83)

This popular day hike follows a moderate grade for 4 miles from the parking area on Cades Cove Loop Road to Abrams Falls. This lower creek trail is often crowded, so do not expect a lot of solitude. The trail generally remains several hundred feet above Abrams Creek and there is one notable climb over a low ridge about half-way to the falls.

Abrams Creek is especially popular with fishermen and the trail provides access to the river at several points if you are willing to scramble down a steep slope. It is probably easiest for fishermen to hike the length of the creek from the upper trailhead near the parking area.

The falls only drop about 20 feet, but there is a large pool beneath the falls. Swimming here is not recommended due to a severe undertow.

Hatcher Mountain Trail (84)

This moderate lowland trail gains 600 feet in nearly 3 miles, wrapping along low dry ridges. The trail connects Abrams Falls Trail (83) with Beard Cane Trail (78). There are few water sources except for one creek, the cool shaded Oak Flats Branch. This would be the best stop for an extended break.

Scott Gap-Abrams Creek Connector Trail (85)

This moderate lowland trail climbs 500 feet in nearly 2 miles to connect Abrams Creek to Scott Gap. The trail rises quickly at first from the river through a beautiful section of moist forest. After this first climb, the trail more gradually wraps around dry ridges to Scott Gap and Scott Gap Campsite #16.

Little Bottoms Trail (86)

This moderate lower creek trail travel 2.3 miles from Abrams Creek Campground to Abrams Falls. The trail becomes very narrow and rugged a couple of miles from the campground, just beyond the heavily-used Little Bottoms Campsite #17. The section before the horse trail below Abrams Falls was the least well-graded trail (as of 1990) that I have seen in the Park!

Rabbit Creek Trail (87)

This moderate lowland trail connects Abrams Creek and Cades Cove. It goes over several small ridges on its way to Abrams Creek Ranger Station and Campground. The eastern end of the trail begins at the parking area for Abrams Falls Trail (83) and the trail immediately crosses the normally-shallow Abrams Creek (no bridge and no large rocks to hop across on).

The first section of trail from the shelter towards Abrams Creek is uphill to the crest of Pine Mountain, then the trail descends very steeply to the creek where there is a log bridge for hikers. The trail follows old roads through a dry mixed pine-oak forest to Rabbit Creek Campsite #15. Then it ascends the ridge through a lush forest to Scott Gap Campsite #16 on Hannah Mountain Trail (88).

Rabbit Creek Campsite is located next to a beautiful section of creek about a mile from Scott Gap Shelter. The shelter is a small, rustic building that has room for eight on wire bunks and is without bear fencing.

Hannah Mountain Trail (88)

This moderate low ridge trail has about an 1,100-foot elevation change in 7.6 miles. The trail connects Gregory Bald or Parsons Branch Road to the Abrams Creek Area. It follows a moderate-grade horse trail. The trail passes through dry stunted oak-pine forest that is occasionally burned by wildfire. There are no water sources along the first 3.5 miles north of Parson Branch Road.

Gregory Bald Trail (89)

This strenuous low ridge trail connects Parsons Branch Road to the main ridge at Sheep Pen Gap Campsite #13 where it rises a steady 2,600 feet in 5.5 miles, then continues 3.1 miles to Doe Knob. The trail offers a second access to Gregory Bald. *Note:* Wolf Ridge Trail (94) out of Twentymile Ranger Station ends at the campsite.

Gregory Ridge Trail (90)

This moderate, 4.9-mile trail climbs 2,000 feet to Gregory Bald from the parking area at the beginning of Parson Branch Road. The lower end of this trail follows Forge Creek, and the trail passes through the most beautiful virgin forest in the Cades Cove Area on its way to the gorgeous Forge Creek Campsite #12.

Then the trail gradually ascends Gregory Ridge to the top of the main ridge, where it opens into a world-famous grass bald noted for its display of flame azaleas during the last two weeks of June. There is an excellent water source, Moore Spring, just south of the ridge's intersection with Gregory Bald Trail (89) along an obvious but unmarked trail.

The Park Service is attempting to manage the bald by selectively cutting down the encroaching trees and seasonally burning the bald. The resulting 360-degree view is one of the best in the Park! There is an especially pretty campsite (Sheep Pen Gap Campsite #13) in the gap between Parson Bald and Gregory Bald. This campsite is routinely visited by bears, so hang your food especially well!

Recommended Hiking

There are numerous day hikes around Cades Cove. I highly recommend Anthony Creek Trail (73), Rich Mountain Loop Trail (75), and Gregory Ridge Trail (90).

Several day hikes and short loops can be taken to connect with trails from Cades Cove or along Beard Cane Trail (78) and Ace Gap Trail (79). Alternate loops can be taken along Hannah Mountain Trail (88) towards Gregory Bald and around Cades Cove. Another loop trail with easy connections to other western areas of the Park is along Beard Cane Trail (78). This extremely easy 4-mile trail can be reached by following Cane Gap Trail (80) from Abrams Creek Campground or by following part of the old Cooper Road Trail (77) from the Cades Cove Loop Road.

There are also numerous possible loops out of Cades Cove. You can ascend the main ridge on Gregory Ridge Trail (90), travel along the low mountains astride the Park's western boundary on Hannah Mountain Trail (88), reach Rich Mountain (use trail 76), circle around the backside of Scott Mountain and Whiteoak Sink (use trail 59), and connect with trails back to the Cades Cove or Tremont Areas. Scott Mountain Trail (59), around the northeast side of Scott Mountain and beyond to Whiteoak Sink, is one of my favorites!

Twentymile Creek-Eagle Creek Areas

The southwestern end of the Smokies contains the easy-to-reach Twentymile Creek Area and the more difficult-to-reach Eagle Creek Area. Area highlights include boating and fishing, trails along rushing streams, and fantastic views from Shuckstack and Gregory Bald. Eagle Creek is the next stream east of Twentymile Creek.

Twentymile-Eagle Creek Areas are located off NC 28 along the southwestern edge of the Park. NC 28 between the Foothills Parkway and Fontana Dam is perhaps the most winding and curvy road in the area! The Dam is located at the end of a short road off NC 28.

Twentymile Ranger Station is located along NC 28 beside Lake Cheoah, west of Fontana Village. Eagle Creek is only accessible by boat across Fontana Lake from Fontana Marina, or by foot along part of the Western Shoreline Trail (95) from Fontana Dam.

Lodging and limited supplies are available nearby at Peppertree Fontana Village Resort (see Appendix C), originally a work camp for the construction of Fontana Dam. Car-camping is available at two National Forest Recreational Areas along Fontana Lake off NC 28: Cable Cove and Tsali.

There are three backcountry sites in the area: Twentymile Creek Campsite #93, Dalton Branch Campsite #95, and Upper Flats Campsite #92. These campsites can be reached by fairly easy, 3- to 5-mile trails.

Trail Descriptions

From Twentymile Creek Ranger Station, several trails lead to Gregory Bald (93 and 94) and to Shuckstack Firetower (91). The trails along the creeks above the ranger station are especially beautiful. Numerous small cascades fall over huge boulders.

Twentymile Creek Trail (91)

This strenuous trail follows the scenic Twentymile Creek from the ranger station to Sassafras Gap, which is about .5 miles from Shuckstack Firetower. It climbs 2,300 feet in 4.5 miles. This trail is the most gradual way to reach the firetower and its impressive views of Lake Fontana.

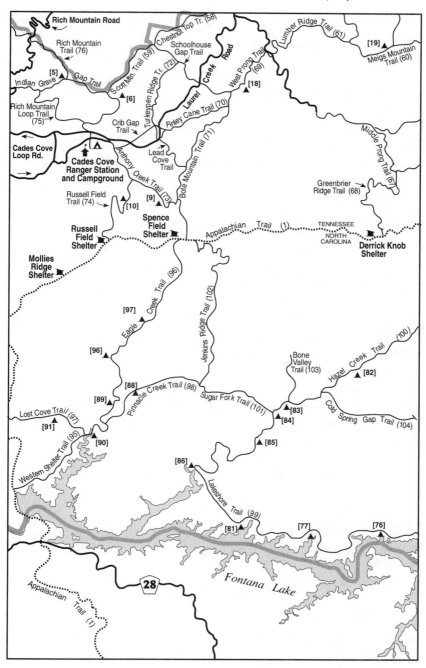

The first 3 miles of trail, which are ideal for day hiking, run gradually along the rushing stream. The last 2 miles climb steadily along a jeep road.

Twentymile Loop Trail (92)
This moderate connector trail climbs 500 feet over the lower end of Long Hungry Ridge. The 2.8-mile trail can be used as part of a loop for a beautiful 8-mile day hike from the ranger station. The prettiest section of this connector trail is along the first mile, west of Twentymile Creek.

Long Hungry Ridge Trail (93)
This strenuous 4.5-mile trail from Twentymile Creek to the ridge below Gregory Bald is especially dazzling, climbing 2,200 feet up through several forest types. Upper Flats Campsite #92 is beautiful and has lots of level tent sites.

The lower half of the trail is very steep, ascending on switchbacks to Rye Patch. The last mile of the trail above Rye Patch is much more gradual, so relax and enjoy it after your hard climb. The best views from this trail are in late fall and winter.

Wolf Ridge Trail (94)
This strenuous, 6.5-mile trail climbs over 2,600 feet to Sheep Pen Gap and Campsite #13. This extremely demanding route consists mostly of high ridge trail. There are numerous switchbacks along the middle section, but the trail is relatively level from Dalton Campsite #95 to Twentymile Creek. The flame azaleas are dazzling along this trail the first two weeks of June.

Western Shoreline Trail (95)
This 5.5-mile lowland trail travels from Fontana Dam to Eagle Creek. It is relatively easy and mostly follows an old road above the lake's shoreline. Numerous abandoned car and truck bodies from the 1930s to early 1940s can been seen. The trail goes up and down several minor side ridges, although elevation changes are usually only a few hundred feet at a time.

Twentymile Creek-Eagle Creek
Backcountry Campsites

Campsite	Number	Elevation	Use	Hikers	Horses
Pinnacle Creek	88	2200	Medium	8	8
Lower Ekaneetlee	89	1880	Medium	8	No
Lost Cove	90	1760	Medium	12	12
Upper Lost Cove	91	2040	Medium	10	10
Upper Flats	92	2520	Medium	14	No
Twentymile Creek	93	1880	Medium	NS	No
Dalton Branch	95	2360	Light	8	8
Eagle Creek	96	2880	Medium	10	No
Big Walnut	97	2400	Light	10	No

Eagle Creek Trail (96)

This moderate lower creek trail follows Eagle Creek and leads to Spence Field Shelter. It climbs over 3,000 feet in 9 miles.

The hike requires 19 stream crossings, either of the main creek or side streams, so plan to get wet. Keep your boots on for better footing. These crossings can be especially dangerous following a heavy rainstorm.

The trail follows old railroad grades that used to have bridges over the many main stream crossings. The bridges are long gone. I have seen a rare beaver dam about half-way up the valley. The upper end of this trail travels through a more open forest with sedge "grass" carpeting the ground. Spence Field is an unequalled open meadow that heavily visited by hikers and bears. Spence Field Shelter is the most heavily used in the Park and it shows much wear and tear. There have been bears around the shelter the last three times I have visited.

Two connector trails lead from the base of Eagle Creek Trail (96) at Lake Fontana: Lost Cove Trail (97) and Pinnacle Creek Trail (98).

Lost Cove Trail (97)

This connector trail, which leaves from the base of Eagle Creek Trail, climbs west to the A.T. at Sassafras Gap on Twentymile Ridge, about .5 miles from Shuckstack Firetower. This 3.5-mile trail is strenuous as it climbs 1,900 feet.

The lower end of the trail is very easy, although there are several small stream crossings before reaching Upper Lost Cove Campsite #91. This pleasant campsite shows little use. This trail is very steep over the last .5 miles.

Pinnacle Creek Trail (98)

This relatively easy lowland trail connects Eagle Creek and Hazel Creek Areas. The moderate trail, which also leaves from the base of Eagle Creek Trail, ascends 1,100 feet in 3.5 miles.

There is a dangerous stream crossing on Eagle Creek at the western end of the trail. The water, raging after a heavy thunderstorm, was thigh deep when I was last there. The trail crosses back and forth across the small Pinnacle Creek and then reaches Pinnacle Creek Campsite #88.

After the campsite, the footpath turns into a wide roadbed built for practice by the U.S. Army Corp of Engineers during the early years of World War II. The road gradually climbs to Jenkins Ridge where it joins Sugar Fork Trail (101) and meets the trailhead of Jenkins Ridge Trail (102).

Jenkins Ridge Trail (102)

This moderate high ridge trail rises 2,000 feet in 6 miles. The first part of the trail is extremely steep, rising about 800 feet during the second half mile! This is the steepest section I can remember of any trail in the Park!

The trail continues more gradually, climbing to Spence Field and the A.T. There is another short, steep section just prior to a small field at Haw Gap (there is a good water source on the trail). The trail then slabs around the ridge where many rocks are exposed in numerous boulder fields.

The trail crosses several small streams including the especially gorgeous Gunna Creek. After this creek, the trail follows an easy grade to the A.T. through a tunnel framed by thick rhododendrons and offers occasional views of Spence Field. The upper end of the trail to Haw Gap would make a wonderful day hike from Spence Field.

Recommended Hiking

The best day hikes in the area include any part of Twentymile Creek Trail (91), the strenuous climb to the view from Shuckstack Firetower, and hikes along Fontana Lake.

A nice 21-mile loop trip can be made starting from the ranger station. Take Wolf Ridge Trail (94) to Gregory Bald, follow Gregory Bald Trail (89) along the crest to Doe Knob, descend along the A.T. to near Shuckstack Firetower, and finally, return along Twentymile Creek Trail (91).

I also recommend a 20.5-mile loop. Go up Long Hungry Ridge Trail (93) to Gregory Bald, back along the crest to Doe Knob, and down to Sassafras Gap below Shuckstack. Return to ranger station.

Middle Creeks:
—Hazel, Forney, and Noland Creeks

The middle creeks have a rich history of previous settlement. There are numerous old overgrown homesites and non-native, evergreen ornamental shrubs and ground cover, such as English boxwood and periwinkle. Several former town sites were flooded by the formation of Fontana Lake.

Middle Creeks Area is reached by following Lakeview Road from downtown Bryson City, located along the southern edge of the Park west of Cherokee. Lakeview Drive is difficult to find, follow signs to the Smoky Mountain Scenic Railroad Station in Bryson City and continue straight across the railroad tracks past the station and high school. Do not follow signs to Deep Creek Campground.

Lakeview Drive winds around low ridges for about 6 miles before it deadends just before a gated tunnel. The Earthwalk Press Map (see Appendix B) is especially useful when traveling the maze of roads around the south shore of Fontana Lake.

Lakeview Drive, locally nicknamed "Road-to-Nowhere," leads to the lower end of Noland Creek. The road ends at a gate about .75 miles west of Noland Creek near a completed, but unused auto

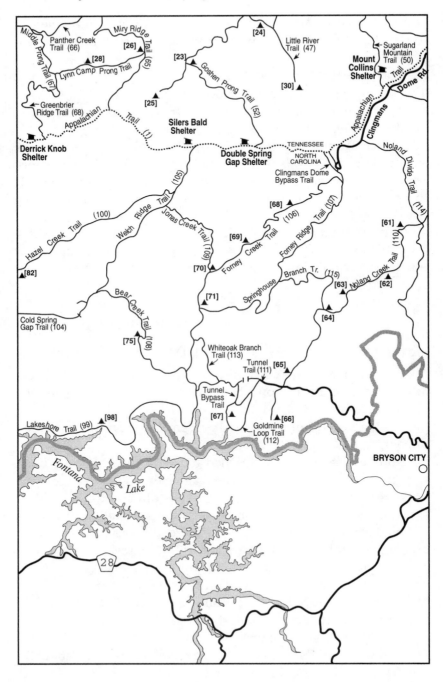

tunnel. You can hike through the tunnel, which offers convenient access to the lower end of Noland Creek and to trails in the nearby Forney Creek Area. This road was started following the flooding of Fontana Lake but was never completed.

The only car-camping in this area of the Park is several miles to the east at Deep Creek Campground or at nearby private campgrounds. Several National Forest Service campgrounds are located across Fontana Lake: Cable Gap and Tsali.

It is easy to boat-in to trailheads and campsites from one of the many marinas or access roads. Boat ferries can be obtained from the Fontana Marina near Fontana Dam, or from several marinas near Bryson City.

There are nine backcountry campsites (#98, #86, #81, #77, #76, #75, #74, #67 and #66) located at the edge of Fontana Lake. Campsites #81, #77, and #76 were previously only accessible by boat but now can be reached using Lakeshore Trail (99).

Trail Descriptions

Most of the lower creek trails follow wide railroad beds that climb gradually up the valleys from Fontana Lake. There are numerous stream crossings without bridges, especially along the upper creek sections. The steams are especially favored by fishermen.

The trails up Forney Ridge (107), Noland Creek (110), and Forney Creek (106) lead to Clingmans Dome and are exceptionally beautiful. There is an average elevation change of 3,000 to 4,000 feet between the lower ends and main ridge. Expect some hard climbs if you head to the A.T.!

From the end of Lakeview Drive, four trails (Lakeshore Trail, Tunnel Trail, Goldmine Loop Trail, and White Oak Branch Trail) allow connection with Forney Creek Trail (107).

Lakeshore Trail (99)

This relatively new lowland trail connects the bottom end of Hazel Creek and Lakeview Drive near Forney Creek. This moderate, 25-mile trail is not intersected by any other trail between Noland and Hazel Creeks, but you can arrange for a boat to go in or be picked up at any of six campsites (#74, #76, #77, #81, #86, #98), which are located beside Fontana Lake.

Kirkland Creek Campsite #76 is near the lake. Pilkey Creek Campsite #77 is one creek west of Pilkey Creek, about .5 miles from the lakeshore. There is one particularly beautiful waterfall and old home site between campsites #81 and #77.

The trail follows old roadways and farm roads for most of its length. You will go up and down the ends of numerous small ridges and you will pass through old farm sites. From the trailhead at the end of Lakeview Drive, the trail loops around the lower end of Tunnel Ridge for nearly 2 miles. If you take Tunnel Trail (111) from the trailhead, you can short-cut over to Lakeshore Trail and save yourself about 1.5 miles.

The trail is confusing to follow at points because there are many odd turns, especially after climbing down the western side of Welch Ridge near Hazel Creek. When in doubt, follow the horse hoofprints!

The climb over Welch Ridge is very steep, requiring a gain of about 700 feet in less than 1 mile. This is the only extremely strenuous climb along the trail and can be quite unexpected after two days of easy hiking!

There is a lot of wildlife in this somewhat isolated section. I recall running into three bear on this trail. These encounters occurred as I was just topping a ridge, so I believe the bear had just not heard me. In every case, the bear bolted away but not before I got a good adrenaline rush!

I have not had bear encounters at any of this trail's campsites, which do not seem to be too frequently used. I hiked this trail for three rainy days without seeing any other hikers, although boat noises were frequent.

Hazel Creek Trail (100)

This trail follows old roads and railroad grades along most of its length. This lower creek and creek headwater trail is moderate and climbs nearly 3,200 feet in 16.5 miles. The Park Service considers the nearly 5-mile long approach trail to Hazel Creek Trail a part of Lakeshore Trail. Trail signs label the 11.8 miles from Sugar Fork to Welch Ridge as Hazel Creek Trail.

Hazel Creek was once heavily populated and was the largest watershed cut by the Ritter Lumber Company in the 1920s and 1930s. The Proctor Campsite #86 sits at the former town of Proctor, which at one time had a population of over a thousand people. The history of Hazel Creek by Duane Oliver, *Hazel Creek—From Then to Now*, is fascinating and can be used as a guide to the old sawmill and logging camps in the area.

The trail follows and crosses (on bridges) Hazel Creek prior to Sugar Fork Campsite #84. This campsite is the prettiest in the area. Horses will need to follow trails that remain on the west side of the creek until Bone Valley Campsite #83. This rationed campsite is heavily used with little privacy.

The trail continues along the creek and is open to horses as far as Calhoun Campsite #82, another former logging camp. The trail continues up to the headwaters of Hazel Creek along a railroad bed but finally leaves the creek to climb steeply up the ridge to end at the Welch Ridge Trail (105), about 1.5 miles from the A.T.

Note: The trailhead of Hazel Creek Trail, which is near the intersection with Welch Ridge, has been recently re-routed. Use care to find the trailhead if you are coming from Welch Ridge because this intersection was poorly marked in 1991.

Sugar Fork Trail (101)
This trail follows entirely along a gradual roadbed. This moderate lowland trail climbs 800 feet in 2.5 miles. For a wonderful place to explore on a day trip, hike this trail from Campsite #84. The trail crests the lower end of Jenkins Ridge where Jenkins Ridge Trail (102) and Pinnacle Creek Trail (98) meet. It passes by numerous old homesites, including one used by the famous writer Horace Kephart.

Jenkins Ridge Trail (102)
This trail is described in the section called Twentymile-Eagle Areas.

Bone Valley Trail (103)
This short deadend side trail off of Hazel Creek is very easy. For 1.5 miles, this lower creek trail rises 100 feet from Hazel Creek to the restored, historical Hall Cabin.

Bone Valley is beautiful, wide, and isolated. It received its name following a late-season snowstorm that killed a herd of cattle. The trail crosses a good-sized stream five times, so plan on wet boots! Especially good trout fishing is reported along this stream.

Middle Creeks Backcountry Campsites

Campsite	Number	Elevation	Use	Hikers	Horses
Bald Creek	61	3560	Medium	12	6
Upper Ripskin	62	3160	Medium	12	6
Jerry Flats	63	2920	Medium	10	6
Mill Creek	64	2540	Medium	20	12
Bear Pen Branch	65	2040	Light	8	8
Lower Noland Creek	66	1720	Light	10	No
Goldmine Branch	67	1840	Light	10	10
Steel Trap	68	3960	Medium	8	No
Huggins	69	2800	Light	12	No
Jons Creek	70	2400	Medium	12	6
CCC	71	2180	Rationed	12	12
Bear Creek	73	1800	Medium	15	6
Lower Forney	74	1720	Medium	12	No
Kirkland Creek	76	1770	Medium		Yes
Pilkey Creek	77	1800	Light		Yes
North Shore	81	1800	Light		Yes
Calhoun	82	2720	Medium	15	10
Bone Valley	83	2280	Rationed	20	10
Sugar Fork	84	2160	Medium	8	8
Sawdust Pile	85	2000	Medium	20	Yes
Proctor	86	1680	Medium	20	12
Chambers Creek	98	1720	Light	10	No

Cold Spring Gap Trail (104)
Farther up Hazel Creek Trail, this trail begins as a connector to Welch Ridge. This strenuous creek headwater trail climbs nearly 2,500 feet in 4 miles. The trail is very rocky, first following a small side creek and then rising to the ridge with one major switchback. There is an important water source below the trail in a boulder field about .25 miles before the intersection with Welch Ridge Trail (105).

Welch Ridge Trail (105)
Near the end of this trail, there is a short side trail to the outlook at High Rocks (elevation 5,200 feet), formerly the location of a firetower and ranger cabin. Good 180-degree views to the southwest include the surrounding valleys towards Fontana Lake and the southern half of the main ridge; trees block the views north and east. Winter views are much better.

This moderate high ridge trail ascends 2,100 feet over 6.5 miles. The trail is easy along most of its length, slabbing across interconnecting ridges with little elevation change for about half its length. The steepest section is the .75-mile section south from the A.T. where the trail climbs steadily through tall briers.

Forney Creek Trail (106)
This strenuous lower creek trail connects Fontana Lake to Clingmans Dome. The 10-mile trail gains over 4,000 feet. Forney Creek is very pretty, especially through the exquisite forest along the upper third of the trail near Clingmans Dome.

The trail crosses the creek frequently in the middle section above Jonas Creek Campsite #70. There are four major stream crossings that make this trail difficult for children. This trail is probably the worst in the Park for total number of difficult stream crossings. Steel Trap Campsite #68 is especially nice.

The lower half of the trail follows along an old railroad bed. All the old railroad bridges are washed out, so when you see any well-worn side trails leading uphill, follow them to avoid having to ford the stream.

Forney Ridge Trail (107)

This moderately strenuous trail drops over 2400 feet in 5.7 miles from Clingmans Dome to the ridgecrest junction with Springhouse Branch Trail (115-116). The upper end leads through dark spruce-fir forest to Andrews Bald, which has been partially cleared affording excellent views to the south and east. The trail then gradually declines down the ridge, intersecting Springhouse Branch Trail (115) along the middle section of the ridge.

Bear Creek Trail (108)

This strenuous trail leads from Forney Creek to the lower end of Welch Ridge Trail near High Rocks. It climbs over 3,000 feet in 6 miles.

For the first 3 miles, the trail follows an easy section of roadway from Forney Creek. It then climbs uphill so steeply at one point that a section was named "The Jump-up" because the trail appears to disappear as it jumps up over a small ridge. There are no water sources along the upper 3 miles.

Jonas Creek Trail (109)

As a second connector from Forney Creek to the upper end of Welch Ridge, this strenuous creek headwater trail ascends 2,200 feet in 4.5 miles. This especially gorgeous trail climbs switchbacks through three vegetation zones prior to reaching the top of Welch Ridge.

The lower half of the trail travels through lush, dense forest near Jonas Creek. Then the trail becomes more open with several good lookouts near the ridge.

Noland Creek Trail (110)

This moderate trail closely follows Noland Creek along most of its length from the main ridge to Fontana Lake. It drops 2,500 over 10.5 miles.

For most of its length, the trail is gradual following old railroad grades until reaching the uppermost campsite, Bald Creek Campsite #61. This is a very pretty, but apparently heavily used, campsite. The trail then turns away from the river to follow a side creek towards Noland Divide. The trail becomes very steep for the last .5 miles prior to reaching Noland Divide Trail (114).

Tunnel Trail (111)

This very easy, .7-mile trail leads from the end of Lakeview Drive through a two-lane auto tunnel. This is the shortest and easiest trail to connect with trails over to Noland Creek. It allows you to cut about 1.5 miles off the Lakeshore Trail, which loops along lower slopes around the end of Tunnel Ridge.

Goldmine Loop Trail (112)

This moderate, 4-mile trail drops about 900 feet to the edge of Fontana Lake. The trail is incorrectly shown to be only 2 miles long on the *1991 Park Trail Map*. There is a campsite, Goldmine Branch Campsite #67, about .5 miles from the lake on a short side trail. The trail mostly follows old roads and passes by old farms and rock chimneys.

White Oak Branch Trail (113)

This moderate, 2-mile lowland trail can be used to reach Forney Creek from Lakeshore Trail (99). The trail drops 400 feet through a series of low gaps to reach Forney Creek about 2 miles upstream of Fontana Lake.

Noland Divide Trail (114)

This fairly gradual trail connects Clingmans Dome Road with Deep Creek Campground. The nearly 12-mile ridge trail ascends over 4,100 feet. Hikers can connect with the A.T. by hiking northeast from the trailhead along Clingmans Dome Road for about .75 miles to Collins Gap. Here, the A.T. runs about 100 feet above the road. *Note:* There is no sign, but it is the only trail seen leading from the road.

The upper end of this trail passes through lush, spruce forest, while the rest of the trail travels through deciduous forest. There are no water sources along most of this trail. There is one nice lookout ("Lonesome Pine") at Beaugard Ridge, about 3.5 miles from Deep Creek Campground. This is a very strenuous climb to the overlook.

Springhouse Branch Trail (115/116)

This is a strenuous, 8.3-mile, ridge hopping trail. It gains nearly 1,400 feet from Noland Creek Trail (110) at campsite #64 to Forney Ridge Trail (107). This section continues up the eastern slope of Forney Ridge past numerous rock piles and through small "pole" timber woods that indicate re-grown fields. The last mile prior to the ridgecrest is through a beautiful old growth forest that is one of the few remaining along the lower southern slopes of the Park. The western section of the trail (formerly Bee Gum Trail) is strenuous, descending to Campsite #71, which was a major Civilian Conservation Corp camp; a huge stone chimney is still standing. The trail gradually descends 1,600 feet using switchbacks to steeply descend to the lower end of Forney Creek Trail, crossing the small creek several times. The hike along the stream is especially beautiful.

Recommended Hiking

Day hikes in the area are mostly limited to trails off Lakeview Drive or from Clingmans Dome Road. From Lakeview Drive, I recommend the easy part of Noland Creek Trail (110), and Tunnel Trail (111) and Goldmine Loop Trail (112). I highly recommend two trails from Clingmans Dome Road—the upper ends of Noland Divide Trail (114) and Forney Ridge Trail (107), which lead to views at Andrews Bald.

Two of my favorite loop trips in this area originate from Clingmans Dome Parking Area. The loops combine ridge and stream trails. Hike down Hazel Creek Trail (100) and return via Welch Ridge (105), or hike down Forney Creek Trail (106) and return via Forney Ridge Trail (107).

The short connector trail above Jonas Creek (use trail 109) from Welch Ridge to Forney Creek is especially beautiful. It wraps around steep ridges and passes through several vegetation zones.

Deep Creek Area

The trail system around Deep Creek offers some of the greatest loop trips of any area of the Park. Deep Creek is especially known for its waterfalls, tubing, and fishing opportunities. Trips on the scenic Smoky Mountain Railroad, which leaves from downtown Bryson City, are offered during the summer.

Deep Creek Area (and campground), located at 1,850 feet, is easily reached by following signs out of Bryson City; watch carefully for three major turns. Bryson City (as well as Cherokee) is most easily reached by following the Smoky Mountain Expressway (US 19 and

US 19/23), which runs along the southern border of the Park from Waynesville to just beyond Bryson City.

Trail Descriptions

There are three major trails ascending to the main ridge and numerous connector trails. There are a half-dozen campsites along the lower end of the valley.

Deep Creek Trail (117)

This trail is well-known among trout fishermen. The trail is moderate and climbs 2,800 feet in nearly 14 miles. This lower creek trail runs mostly along old railroad grades with no bridges above Campsite #53. Along the trail, there are eight backcountry campsites, more or less evenly spaced up and down the river.

There are four major side ridges that lead down to the east side of the creek. When these ridges intersect Deep Creek, the trail climbs up away from the creek on well-worn side trails to avoid stream fording. You should follow all of these routes.

The headwaters of Deep Creek are extremely beautiful, forming suddenly out of a thick hemlock forest near Newfound Gap Road. The trail passes through a magnificent hardwood forest for 4 miles before reaching Poke Patch Campsite #53. All the campsites along the river are regularly visited by bear in the summer, so be sure to hang your food extremely well.

Pole Road Creek Trail (118)

This exceptionally charming trail connects Noland Divide and Deep Creek. This strenuous creek headwater trail climbs 1,800 feet in less than 3.5 miles, using switchbacks through lush forest with huge hemlocks. The lower half of the trail crosses Pole Road Creek three times without bridges, but the area is so beautiful I hardly mind wet feet. There is no water along the upper mile of this trail or on the nearby Noland Divide.

Fork Ridge Trail (119)

This trail leads from Poke Patch Campsite #53 to Clingmans Dome Road and the A.T. near Mt. Collins Shelter. The trail is strenuous and climbs nearly 3,000 feet in about 5 miles.

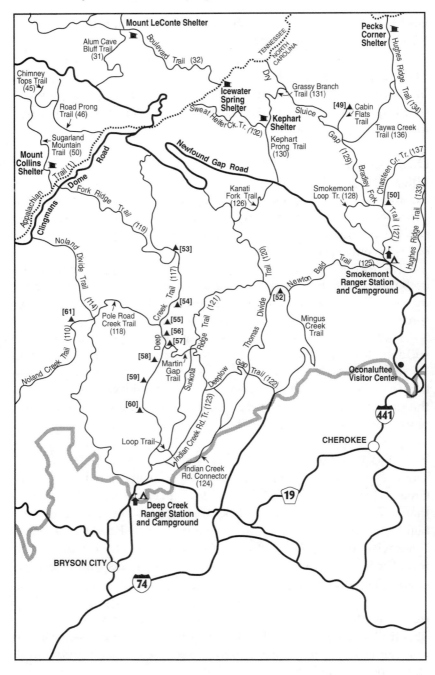

From Deep Creek, the trail climbs quickly up a low ridge and ascends to an exceptionally beautiful hemlock grove. The trail continues upward with one great switchback to reach the main shoulder of Fork Ridge. From here to Clingmans Dome Road, the trail passes through an extremely beautiful spruce forest carpeted with ferns and wild sorrel. I highly recommend the upper half of this trail for an exceptional, albeit strenuous, day hike.

Thomas Divide Trail (120)

This trail joins Newton Bald Trail (125) a short distance from Newton Bald Campsite #52 and is highly recommended, especially during late winter and early spring when leafless trees allow superb views. The trail is moderate and ascends 2,600 feet in nearly 14 miles.

The lower part of the trail follows along the graded roadbed of a canceled auto route (part of the proposed Indian Creek Road). The trail ascends gradually along this wide road for 3 miles, leaves the road to ascend along a narrow ridge trail to Deeplow Gap, and crosses Deeplow Gap Trail (122).

From here, the trail steeply climbs around ridges with numerous lookouts during the last mile and reaches Newton Bald Trail (125) and nearby Newton Bald Campsite #52. From this intersection, the trail runs along an easy grade to intersect with Kanati Fork Trail (126). The trail then follows an especially beautiful, narrow, and nearly level ridge for 2 miles through open forest carpeted with evergreen sedge-grass.

The last 1.7-mile section of trail, from the big hairpin curve along Newfound Gap Road about 3.5 miles south of Newfound Gap, would make an excellent short day hike. The trailhead is marked as a Quiet Walkway near Webb Overlook.

Sunkota Ridge Trail (121)

This trail follows along the narrow, low-elevation Sunkota Ridge, which separates Deep Creek from Indian Creek. The moderate trail climbs 2,800 feet in nearly 9 miles. There are no water sources along this trail and there are few views except in winter. The upper half of this trail winds along a connecting ridge that was damaged by fire in the late 1980s, scorched tree trunks are common. Martin Gap Trail and Indian Creek Road Trail (123) allow access to the middle section

Deep Creek Backcountry Campsites

Campsite	Number	Elevation	Use	Hikers	Horses
Newton Bald	52	5000	Medium	8	8
Poke Patch	53	3000	Medium	12	No
Nettle Creek	54	2600	Light	8	No
Pole Road	55	2410	Rationed	15	15
Burnt Spruce	56	2405	Medium	10	10
Bryson Place	57	2360	Rationed	20	12
Nicks Nest Branch	58	2360	Medium	6	6
McCracken Branch	59	2320	Light	6	6
Bumgardner Branch	60	2120	Medium	10	10

of Sunkota Ridge Trail, allowing a potential loophike from Deep Creek Campground.

Deeplow Gap Trail (122)

This moderate trail connects Indian Creek with Newton Bald. It climbs 2,500 feet in less than 9 miles. The trail first ascends to Deeplow Gap and then drops to Little Creek Falls, which consists of layered rocks where the water cascades and splashes wildly at each level.

Next, the trail meanders through a beautiful, small valley where grassy meadows and black walnut trees indicate abandoned farms. Finally, the trail climbs steadily to Newton Bald and Newton Bald Campsite #52.

Indian Creek Road Trail (123)

This moderate lower creek trail climbs 1,500 feet in 4.5 miles. It follows almost entirely along a gravel road for over 3.5 miles, then travels steep switchbacks up to Martin Gap along the middle section of Sunkota Ridge. A 1.5-mile Martin Gap Trail connects the middle of Sunkota Ridge to Deep Creek Trail (117) at Campsite #57.

The trail is quite beautiful along its upper section, curving gracefully in and out of small stream gullies. The last available water is about 1.5 miles below the gap.

Indian Creek Road Connector Trail (124)

This lowland trail connects Thomas Divide Trail (120) and Indian Creek Road Trail (123). Although it follows along a roadbed, the trail is strenuous because it descends 1,000 feet in 2 miles. The descent passes through several old farm sites.

Recommended Hiking

Recommended day hikes include trails around the Deep Creek Campground. There are numerous waterfalls in the area, but the best (and least publicized) is Little Creek Falls, located on Deeplow Gap Trail (122) about 5 miles from the campground.

For a nice day hike to these falls, take Indian Creek Road Trail (123) to Deeplow Gap Trail (122), ascend to Deeplow Gap (elevation 3,700 feet) on Thomas Ridge, and continue down about .5 miles to the falls. To return to the campground on a different trail, follow the lower part of Thomas Divide Trail (120) back to Indian Creek Road.

From Clingmans Dome Road, I highly recommend trails around the upper end of Deep Creek, including Noland Divide Trail (114), Deep Creek Trail (117), Fork Ridge Trail (119), and Thomas Divide Trail (120).

There are many possibilities for backpacking loops in the area. I highly recommend combining Thomas Divide Trail (120) and Deep Creek Trail (117), although this will require about 2 miles of road walking along the busy Newfound Gap Road.

A long loop around the entire watershed would be rewarding, especially if it included Thomas Divide Trail (120), Fork Ridge Trail (119), or Pole Road Branch Trail (118).

Bradley Fork-Raven Fork-_____ Straight Fork Areas

The last area in the Park contains trails along three south-flowing creeks: Bradley Fork, Raven Fork, and Straight Fork of the Oconaluftee River. Area highlights include tubing near the campgrounds and numerous day hikes and backpacking loops.

Bradley Fork parallels the southern half of Newfound Gap Road following the geological Oconaluftee Fault Valley and passing by Smokemont Campground. The next major stream to the east is Raven Fork. This area is considered one of the wildest areas of the Park. The last stream draining south from the Park before Balsam Mountain is Straight Fork.

Bradley Fork-Raven Fork-Straight Fork Areas are reached from Newfound Gap Road (US 441) in the middle of the Park. The trails in the Bradley Fork Area begin at Smokemont Campground and Ranger Station north of Cherokee, just a few miles north of the Oconaluftee Visitor Center.

Raven Fork and Straight Fork are most accessible from Big Cove Road, which passes through the Qualla Cherokee Indian Reservation northeast of Cherokee. Follow signs to the Cherokee Trout Hatchery where the beginning of Straight Fork Road is gated. This road was washed out in 1992 and is expected to be closed for several years, but you can hike along the closed road to reach the trails.

Tubing the Bradley Fork is a popular summer event. There are nearby horse stables on Towstring Road. Also nearby, there is the restored pioneer homestead at Oconaluftee Visitor Center, a seasonally-operated grain mill at Mingus Mill, and a large picnic area at Collins Creek.

Car-camping is available in the area at two Park campgrounds, Smokemont and Balsam Mountain. There are numerous private campgrounds around Cherokee and Maggie Valley. Smokemont Campground (elevation 2,200 feet) is the second largest and second busiest in the Park and is open all year. The campground is about 3 miles north of the Oconaluftee Visitor Center on Newfound Gap Road.

Smokemont Campground is at the site of a former logging camp.

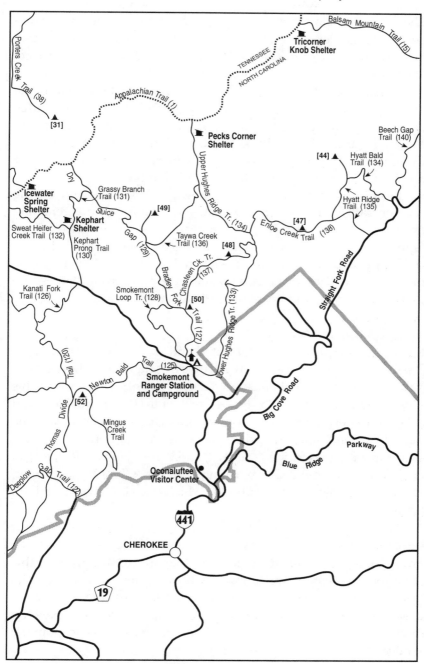

The mountain slopes to the north and west of Smokemont were heavily logged except along the very upper reaches of the creeks. Most of the present forest consists of lovely, moderate-sized, second-growth trees and understory shrubs.

Balsam Mountain Campground is easily accessible by way of the 8-mile paved Heintooga Ridge Road, which is off the Blue Ridge Parkway at milepost 458. Extreme flooding in 1992 closed Balsam Mountain and Straight Fork Roads, isolating Balsam Mountain Campground. These roads have been reopened and Balsam Mountain is once again linked to Smokemont.

Because Balsam Mountain Campground is small and off the "beaten path," it is one of my favorites. The campground (generally open from mid-May through October) is the highest in the Park (approximate elevation 5,400 feet) and is especially pleasant when summer heat drives mere mortals from the valleys below. From the picnic area at Heintooga Overlook (near the campground), there are grand views west and north towards the main ridge.

Trail Descriptions
Raven Fork Area is the most isolated and wildest watershed in the Park and maintained trails only encircle this high valley or deadend half-way up the mountain slopes. There are only four trails in this area: Hyatt Ridge Trail (135), Enloe Creek Trail (138), Hyatt Bald Trail (139), and Beech Gap Trail (140). This is perhaps the best area of the Park if you seek solitude and solidarity with wild nature.

Lower Hughes Ridge Trail (133) and Upper Hughes Ridge Trail (135) link Smokemont Campground with the A.T. at Pecks Corner, and with the Enloe Creek Trail (138), which leads into the Raven Fork Area.

Newton Bald Trail (125)
From Newfound Gap Road near Smokemont Campground, this strenuous trail steadily climbs nearly 3,000 feet in 6 miles. The exceptionally beautiful trail gradually winds across the headwaters of several creeks before more steeply climbing a side ridge. Newton Bald is overgrown with trees and there are few views except in the winter.

Bradley Fork-Smokemont-Raven Fork Backcountry Campsites

Campsite	Number	Elevation	Use	Hikers	Horses
McGhee Spring	44	5040	Medium	12	12
Enloe Creek	47	3620	Rationed	8	8
Upper Chasteen	48	3320	Medium	8	No
Cabin Flats	49	3060	Medium	20	20
Lower Chasteen	50	2360	Rationed	15	15

There are no dependable water sources along the trail's upper 3 miles. The water source at Newton Bald Campsite #52 is variable, so check with rangers to determine if the spring is running or if rainfall has been below normal.

Kanati Fork Trail (126)
This very strenuous, 3-mile trail links Newfound Gap Road and Thomas Divide. It rises 2,100 feet in 3 miles. From the road, the trail climbs along a steady grade through a beautiful cove forest that contains mixed hardwood trees and sections of large hemlocks.

Bradley Fork Trail (127)
From Smokemont Campground, this trail follows a gravel road alongside the fast-flowing Bradley Fork. The trail is rated moderate because it only gains 900 feet in 5 miles. The road allows easy access to several side trails that lead to surrounding ridge trails, including connections to Raven Fork, the A.T., and Deep Creek.

The last mile of Bradley Fork Trail, which leads to Cabin Flats Campsite #49, is heavily mired by horse traffic. The campsite is not rationed but appears to be heavily used. I have found the campsite trashy at times with numerous animal trails. Hang your food high!

Smokemont Loop Trail (128)
This moderate lowland trail ascends 1,200 feet in 5.5 miles to the top of a low ridge. It makes a lovely day hike and wildflower trail out of

Smokemont Campground. The trail begins along Bradley Fork Trail (127), about 1.7 miles from the gate at the head of Smokemont Campground.

Hiking the loop counterclockwise, the trail switchbacks up the lower slope of Richland Mountain through several different forest types and reaches the dry ridge of the lower end of Richland Mountain. Here, there are limited views up the main valley of the Oconaluftee Fault.

The trail then descends steeply on switchbacks before passing the interesting Bradley family cemetery, which is just before the lower end of the campground. I highly recommend hiking this loop counterclockwise as described because it avoids the steep climb above the cemetery.

Dry Sluice Gap Trail (129)

This strenuous high ridge trail rises 2,500 feet in 4 miles from Bradley Fork to the A.T. From the creek, the trail climbs steadily up along numerous switchbacks. After gaining the lower ridge of Richland Mountain, the trail continues to climb steadily to the intersection of Grassy Branch Trail (131).

The last mile of trail to Dry Sluice Gap (just east of Charlies Bunion) is relatively flat with numerous gray snags of dead fir trees. There are a couple of lookouts towards the main ridge and views to the south and over the surrounding slopes.

Kephart Prong Trail (130)

This mostly lower creek trail makes a very suitable, short day hike. The trail is rated strenuous because it climbs 800 feet in 2 miles. It leaves from Newfound Gap Road and follows along a gravel jeep road. There is a large bridge across the Oconaluftee River at the trailhead.

The trail ends at Kephart Shelter, which is at the junction of Sweat Heifer Trail (132) and Grassy Branch Trail (131). This area was once an important lumber camp, and although the entire area was heavily logged, a beautiful forest has now grown back.

Kephart Shelter is heavily used and is well-known for the presence of aggravating "no-see-ems," which are most annoying just after sunrise. Mice seem to love shredding toilet paper, so hang yours with the food.

Grassy Branch Trail (131)

This is a moderately strenuous 2.5-mile trail rises 1700 feet from Kephart Shelter to the crest of Richland Mountain. The lower half of the trail winds around the base of side ridges before becoming much steeper prior to reaching the ridgecrest and Dry Sluice Gap Trail (129). There is a reliable water source about 500 feet below the crest.

Sweat Heifer Creek Trail (132)

This strenuous, 3.7-mile trail ascends 2,300 feet, connecting Kephart Shelter to the main ridge and A.T. From the shelter, the trail climbs gradually for 2 miles along an old railroad grade that circles up and around the large cove of Sweat Heifer Creek.

Two exceptional waterfalls flow across the trail. Use extra care at these creek crossings because the mist from the falls makes the rocks extremely slippery. The lower waterfall is the best place for a break.

Shortly after the second waterfall, the trail leaves the railroad grade and continues steadily upward through beautiful cherry and beech forest. The upper end of this trail was heavily overgrown with briers when I was there last in 1991.

Lower Hughes Ridge Trail (133)

This beautiful connector trail links Bradley Fork Trail (127) and Hughes Ridge. It is a moderate low ridge trail that rises 2,700 feet in 7.3 miles. While parts of this trail are exceptional, it is not highly recommended because it is poorly marked where it temporarily leaves the Park.

For about 1 mile, the trail crosses a small logged section of the Qualla Indian Reservation. Numerous logging roads cross the trail, making the route very confusing. Generally keep to the trail that leads up and circles around the western side of the logged area (follow the horse hoofprints!).

After re-entering the Park, the trail steadily ascends a narrow ridge and reaches a single, short switchback that climbs to a long, nearly-level ridge. The trail is very pleasant for the next few miles, but there are few lookouts because of dense forest.

There are a couple of water sources along this section of ridge trail, about 4 miles from the trailhead at Smokemont. The second stream from the bottom is in an exceptionally pretty valley.

Upper Hughes Ridge Trail (134)

This trail begins on the ridge at the end of Chasteen Creek Trail. This moderate high ridge trail gradually climbs 1,000 feet in nearly 5 miles to Pecks Corner on the A.T.

The trail passes the trailhead of Enloe Creek Trail (138) after about .5 miles and continues to gradually ascend through open forest. For the last two miles, before Pecks Corner Shelter, the trail travels through an exceptionally gorgeous evergreen spruce-fir forest.

Hyatt Ridge Trail (135)

This strenuous trail begins at Straight Fork Road and leads in a big zigzag to Hyatt Bald. This combination creek headwater and low ridge trail climbs 2,000 feet in 4 miles.

From the road, the first mile is gradual, then the trail climbs steadily for about 1,000 feet along a very rocky jeep trail to Low Gap, where it turns sharply to the right. After a very steep climb, the trail becomes more gradual, gaining an additional 600 feet over the next 2.5 miles and reaching the intersection with Hyatt Bald Trail.

McGhee Springs Campsite #44 is one of my favorites; it consists of a one-acre open area surrounded by huge trees. The spring is wonderful! There is usually recent "bear-sign" (broken food-hanging cords, teeth-punctures, trash, etc.) in the campsite, so hang your food extra high.

Near the campsite, an unmaintained (but flagged with plastic ribbon) path extends along Breakneck Ridge. This man-way leaves the side ridge and descends precariously to the headwaters of Raven Fork near the area called Three Forks.

Three Forks Area was considered one of the most beautiful areas in the Park by early Park writers, but all trails into the area are now overgrown. This man-way is very difficult and not recommended for general use. The upper valley of Raven Fork is a traditional Cherokee spiritual center.

Taywa Creek Trail (136)

This beautiful connector trail links Bradley Fork Trail (127) and Hughes Ridge. It begins at the upper end of Bradley Creek Road. This strenuous creek headwater trail climbs 2,100 feet in 3.3 miles.

From Bradley Creek, the trail follows a gradual jeep road for about 1 mile to a stream, which is the last source of water for this trail. From here, the trail climbs steeply on switchbacks for 2 miles to reach the crest of Hughes Ridge and Upper Hughes Ridge Trail (135).

Chasteen Creek Trail (137)

Recommended as the preferred trail from Smokemont Campground to Hughes Mountain Ridge, this strenuous creek headwater trail rises 2,300 feet in 4 miles. It begins at Bradley Fork Trail (127), about 1 mile from Smokemont Campground, immediately before Lower Chasteen Creek Campsite #50. The first 3 miles of this trail are heavily used by horses and may be quite muddy in places. The trail passes a beautiful waterfall about 1 mile beyond Campsite #50 and follows a gradual jeep road to the not-rationed Upper Chasteen Campsite #48.

While both campsites are especially beautiful, with lush ferns and mosses carpeting the stream banks, there are few level tent sites. The backcountry campsites near Smokemont (especially #50 and #48) are known to have frequent bear problems, so hang your food exceptionally well! After the campsite, the trail climbs steadily and is very steep with several switchbacks during the last mile.

Enloe Creek Trail (138)

This is the only trail directly linking Bradley Fork and Raven Fork Areas. This moderate trail drops 1,200 feet in 3.5 miles. From the trailhead on Hughes Ridge, the trail is at first gradual, circling around a connecting ridge and dropping steeply on switchbacks to cross Enloe Creek.

The trail becomes narrow but remains relatively gradual for 1.5 miles to Enloe Creek Campsite #47. The campsite is located on a narrow shelf above the raging Raven Fork. This is a magnificently scenic campsite, overlooking huge boulders in the river below. Beautiful swimming holes are enticing, but the water is so cold that you probably will not stay in for long!

There is a new horse bridge across the river. The trail ascends from the river along a wide muddy jeep trail to Low Gap and the intersection with Lower Hyatt Ridge Trail (134).

Hyatt Bald Trail (139)

This trail links Hyatt Bald and the nearby McGhee Springs Campsite #44 with Straight Fork Road at Round Bottom Parking Area. This strenuous but gradual trail climbs 1,900 feet in nearly 3 miles. The very pretty trail ascends to a side ridge from Hyatt Bald, then turns to circle along a nearly-level route around the summit to Lower Hyatt Ridge Trail. The trail continues along a narrow ridge for a half mile to McGhee Springs. Hyatt Bald is now overgrown, but there are some spectacular views from the ridge into the valleys of Raven Fork and Straight Fork a thousand or more feet below.

Beech Gap Trail (140)

This strenuous, 4.5-mile trail connects Balsam Mountain Trail (15) and Round Bottom Parking Area on Straight Fork Road. The trail descends very steeply from Beech Gap, dropping nearly 3,000 feet along old railroad grade. The last mile of this trail near Round Bottom is unmercifully steep. There are no dependable water sources along this trail.

Recommended Hiking

Highly recommended day hikes in the area include Smokemont Loop Trail (128), Kephart Prong Trail (130), and Chasteen Creek Trail (137).

Numerous loop trips can be planned in this area. An especially beautiful 40-mile loop starts at Smokemont Campground. Take Bradley Fork Trail (127) to Taywa Creek Trail (136), then go up Hughes Ridge (use trail 135) to Pecks Corners. Hike along the A.T. to Tricorner Knob and then along Balsam Mountain Trail (15), Beech Gap Trail (140), and Hyatt Bald Trail (139) to McGhee Springs. Continue along Hyatt Ridge Trail (135), Enloe Creek Trail (138), and Chasteen Creek Trail (137) back to Smokemont.

4
Other Recreation

Scenic Drives

The most popular activity in the Park is automobile touring. The major roads and scenic drives are discussed in Part I. There is an auto map in the free pamphlet, *Great Smoky Mountains*, which can be obtained from visitor centers.

The inexpensive pamphlets produced by the GSMNHA, *Auto Touring* and *Mountain People*, are more detailed guides to the roads through the Park. The Park's official road guide, *Mountain Roads and Quiet Places*, offers additional information including roadside mileposts designating points of interest. I also recommend the series of self-guiding booklets, *Cades Cove Auto Tour*, *Cataloochee Auto Tour*, *Roaring Fork Auto Tour*, and *Oconaluftee Pioneer Farmstead Guide*. These are available for a small fee from roadside boxes at the beginning of the tours, from visitor centers, and by mail from the GSMNHA (see Appendix B).

Historical Sites

For tourists interested in local history, there are wonderful displays in several areas of the Park. The Park staff takes pride in development of historical exhibits and rebuilt farm structures.

Cades Cove contains the best collection of reconstructed pioneer buildings in the Southern Appalachians. The exhibits tell the story of the early mountain settlers. There is also an interesting museum, an operating water mill, and several reconstructed farms and churches along Cades Cove Loop Road.

At Oconaluftee Visitor Center, there is a reconstructed pioneer homestead. Nearby, you will find Mingus Mill, a seasonally operated undershot water mill. Roaring Fork Auto Road, a popular, self-guided route near Gatlinburg, leaves from Cherokee Orchard Parking Area, where there are signs describing some of the natural history and settlements of the area.

In the Cataloochee Area, there are numerous reconstructed homes, barns, and churches. The first weekend of August, the Palmer family holds their annual homecoming. The descendants of the original settlers meet for church services, covered dish meals, and tall tale-telling.

Picnicking

Picnicking is allowed almost anywhere in the Park, and it is a very popular activity. You can pull off the road anywhere there is a designated parking area. Cars are not allowed in fields or on roadsides except where there is an obvious place to park.

There are nine picnicking areas with tables, trash cans, and toilets. Chimney's Picnic Area is open year-round and has 89 sites. Additional picnicking areas are only open from April to November: Cades Cove (81 sites), Look Rock (51 sites), Metcalf Bottoms (165 sites), Cosby (95 sites), Greenbrier (12 sites), Collins Creek (182 sites), Deep Creek (182 sites), and Heintooga (41 sites).

Fishing

Fishing opportunities are great along the over 700 miles of Park streams and lakes. A free brochure, *Fishing Regulations*, which describes current fishing regulations and restrictions, is available at ranger stations. I have found the book *Smoky Mountain Trout Fishing Guide* by Don Kirk (new edition, 1993) to be the best reference on individual areas, specific streams, and recommended fishing flies and gear.

No fishing license is required in the Park for children under the age of 16. The only license required by adults is a regular North Carolina or Tennessee state fishing license. The daily limit is five fish, and the minimum size is seven inches, except for rock bass which has no minimum size restriction. Only artificial lures with a single hook may be used in the Park. Brook trout are a protected species and must be returned to the stream.

There are over 70 species of fish in the Park, but only four are considered game fish: rainbow trout, brown trout, small-mouth bass, and rock bass. The preferred game fish is the introduced rainbow trout. The best streams for this fish are Little River, Abrams Creek, Hazel Creek, Oconaluftee River, and Bradley Fork. Prime fishing spots for rainbow trout are turbulent waters, especially below cascades.

Brown trout are more commonly found in the Little River near Elkmont, and in Big Creek and Oconaluftee River. It is best to fish for brown trout in late evening or early morning.

According to several sources, Abrams Creek draining from Cades Cove is the best stream for trout because of the limestone bedrock and aquatic vegetation. Other highly recommended southeastern trout streams are found on the North Carolina slopes: Eagle Creek, Forney Creek, Noland Creek, and Deep Creek.

Record-size bass are primarily found in shaded pools along the lower elevations. Fontana Lake, especially around the coves and land points, is famous for producing record-size bass.

Some streams and headwaters are closed to fishing under the management of Park officials. These closed areas will be clearly marked. Four streams are closed to all fishing: Mingus Creek, Lands Creek, Chestnut Creek, and LeConte Creek above the intersection with Twin Creek.

Fishing is big business on the Cherokee Reservation. The streams are heavily stocked with large trout and other fishermen! Several fishing contests are conducted each year; prize money runs in the hundreds of dollars. You will need a special Cherokee Reservation Fishing License to fish those streams.

--- Bicycling

Bicycling is most popular in Cades Cove, where bikes can be rented for exploring Cades Cove Loop Road. The road is closed to cars on Saturday mornings until 10:00 A.M. so that you can enjoy traffic-free riding. A variety of animals are attracted to the fields in the Cove, especially early in the morning.

Bikes always have the right-of-way, but you may feel crowded by the thousands of cars that use this beautiful road from 10 A.M. to dark. Biking is allowed on all roads open to vehicles, and there are numerous gravel roads that are not as heavily used. Bikes are not allowed on any trails or gated roads unless specifically marked for bicycle use.

Bicycle touring and mountain biking opportunities have greatly increased in the Southern Appalachian Mountains. The scenic Blue Ridge Parkway is well-known as a major bicycling route in the region. I highly recommend Elizabeth and Charlie Skinner's book, *Bicycling the Blue Ridge*.

Sections of the Mountains-to-the-Sea Bicycling Highway have been completed in western North Carolina. Information on over 3,000 miles of lightly-traveled country roads are available from the North Carolina Department of Transportation. The extremely well-prepared packets include route descriptions, points of interest, maps, public and private campground addresses, and local bike repair services. Map packets are also available for the "Southern Highlands" and "Mountain Connectors."

A series of additional bikeways have been completed in northern Georgia. For information, contact the Georgia Department of Transportation (see Appendix C).

Interest in mountain biking has skyrocketed in the area. Jim Parham has published a wonderful book, *Off the Beaten Track: A Guide to Mountain Biking in Western North Carolina*, that includes details and maps on 25 routes. I understand that Parham has recently produced a second list of bike trails.

Bird Watching

Bird watching is another popular recreation activity in the Park. The Park has a lot of different birds due to its diversity of habitats and elevations, and its location along major migration routes. There is a detailed bird checklist available at visitor centers and campgrounds.

An excellent and inexpensive pocket guide called *Birds of the Great Smoky Mountains National Park* was written by George Stevenson and covers the birds of the area. Stevenson indicates the seasons and common locations (areas and elevations) for the over 200 species of Park birds (70 species are year-round residents). Stevenson divides his list into two groups: birds found below 3,500 feet and birds found above 3,500 feet.

Tubing and Paddling

Tubing is especially popular with the young-at-heart. Prime tubing is enjoyed on the streams around Deep Creek and Smokemont Campgrounds, and along the lower end of Greenbrier Creek. Tubing is also popular from the Townsend Wye on the Little River near Townsend. Tubes, rafts, and life preservers can be rented from nearby entrepreneurs, generally located immediately downstream of the Park boundaries.

Most Park streams are too rocky and shallow for kayaks and canoes. The Little River is the only place were kayakers are commonly seen in the Smokies. Fontana Lake is a great place to canoe.

Whitewater Rafting

The rivers that flow out of the Southern Appalachian Mountains form some of the best whitewater in the eastern United States. Blessed with high rainfall, rapid elevation changes, and an abundance of camping spots in nearby pristine national forests, the region's streams are well-known for river sports, which includes whitewater rafting, kayaking, tubing, and canoeing.

Recreational opportunities are centered along the mountain's major rivers: Nantahala, Ocoee, Chattooga, Tuckaseegee, and French

Broad. The National Forest Service has estimated that 350,000 people will use the first three of these during a single year.

Because people use rivers primarily during the summer, river outfitters have begun to diversify their services and offer additional recreation such as backpacking and cycling trips. Outfitters are also promoting public information about responsible tourism and environmental and resource education.

The Nantahala Outdoor Center (NOC) is a well-known whitewater adventure company located in the Nantahala Gorge at Wesser. The employee-owned NOC offers exciting rafting trips and rafting and kayaking instruction on the Nantahala River. They also organize trips on other rivers in the East, as well as numerous trips around the world.

NOC operates several great restaurants and a store specializing in rafting and backpacking supplies. The A.T. crosses the Nantahala River near NOC and long-distance hikers (myself included and by special request) have been delighted to be served great fresh salads for breakfast—especially delicious after two weeks on the A.T.

The addresses of NOC and other regional whitewater outfitters are listed in Appendix C.

Horseback Riding

Many Park visitors love riding horses. Saddle horses and guided tours are available between April and the end of October from private outfitters at Cades Cove, Smokemont, Duddle Creek, Cosby, and Twomile Branch near Gatlinburg (see Appendix C).

Not all backcountry trails are open to horses. *The Great Smoky Mountain Trail Map* distinguishes between "Hiking Only" trails and "Horse and Hiking" trails. Most of the A.T. in the Park is closed to horses except between Twentymile Trail and Spence Field, and between Pecks Corner and Davenport Gap.

There are five auto-access horse camps (see listing in Part I). Backcountry sites open to horses are listed in Part III. These campsites often have hitching racks and a few of the sites have primitive feeding stalls.

_Cross-Country Skiing and Sledding

Popular winter activities include cross-country skiing and sledding. Many Park roads are closed after the first heavy snow. Clingmans Dome Road is popular with cross-country skiers, and the upper end of Chimneys Picnic Area is popular with sledders. Other roads frequently used by skiers and sledders include: Little River Truck Trail, Roaring Fork Motor Road, and the old Newfound Gap Road.

Appalachian Trail

The A.T. offers numerous recreational opportunities north and south of the Park. The trail through Georgia and North Carolina contains many ascents and descents of 1,000 to 2,000 feet (up and down, up and down).

The A.T. south of the Park runs 160 miles from its southern terminus on Springer Mountain (Georgia) to Fontana Dam. The section in Georgia has many deep gaps and incredible forests of poison ivy, and the climb out of Bly Gap, on the Georgia-North Carolina line is especially strenuous.

Standing Indian Mountain, one of the most prominent peaks in the Southern Appalachians, lies just north of the North Carolina border and offers hiking between 4,000 and 5,000 feet with occasional patches of northern birch forests. Standing Indian Recreational Area has a campground and nearby horse camps, loop trails for trips averaging one to four days, and numerous day hikes. This area receives one of the highest amounts of rainfall in the East, averaging over 80 inches per year.

From the summit of Standing Indian Mountain, the A.T. runs over and along connecting ridges towards the Smokies and passes through the deep Nantahala River Gorge. The climb out of the Nantahala Gorge from Wesser is strenuous, and from here to the Smokies is one of the most frustrating sections of the A.T. because the trail goes up and over every small peak. At least there are free hot showers in the outside restrooms at the Dam!

The A.T. north of the Park crosses the main ridges of the Unaka and Iron Mountain Ranges. Because the trail follows the North Carolina-Tennessee line nearly to Virginia, there is a lot of fence-hopping. The balds at Max Patch and near Roan Mountain offer exceptional views. The section of the A.T. north of the Park is considerably easier than hiking along the A.T. south of the Park.

The Appalachian Trail Conference (see Appendix C) offers a set of guides with trail descriptions and milage. The books include information on water sources and nearby towns, stores, and post offices.

_____Other Long Distance Trails

Three other long distance trails are being developed in northern Georgia and western North Carolina. Approximately 90 miles of the Bartram Trail has been completed near the Smokies. This trail generally follows the route of the early naturalist, William Bartram, who journeyed through the states in the late 1770s. For additional information, contact the North Carolina Bartram Trail Society (see Appendix C).

The Mountains-to-the-Sea Trail will eventually run about 700 miles from Manteo (on the Atlantic Coast) to the Great Smokies. Sections along the Black Mountains and the Blue Ridge Parkway are currently being blazed, but this trail is not yet linked to the Park. For information about the sections following the Blue Ridge Parkway, contact the Carolina Hiking Club, and for information on the entire trail, contact the North Carolina Department of Natural Resources (see Appendix C).

The Benton MacKaye Trail is currently being developed and it will criss-cross the A.T. from Springer Mountain to the Smokies and make various loop trips possible. This trail is presently complete through Georgia to the Tennessee line and is proposed to enter the Smokies and end on Mt. Sterling. For more information, contact the Benton MacKaye Trail Association (see Appendix C).

_____Other Regional Trails

An excellent and inexpensive map/guide, *100 Favorite Trails of the Great Smokies and Carolina Blue Ridge* (see Appendix B), includes hiking trails both in and outside the Park. Compiled by the Carolina Mountain Club and the Smoky Mountain Hiking Club, it is the best at-a-glance map of regional hiking and backpacking trails and contains concise up-to-date detailed reference for 1,700 miles of trail in western North Carolina.

The Great Smoky
Mountain Railroad

The Great Smoky Mountain Railroad, a new attraction that now stops in Wesser on trips originating in Andrews, Bryson City, and Dillsboro, features enclosed or open-air touring cars. You can ride through the beautiful Nantahala Gorge and along sections of Fontana Lake. Generally, there are two daily excursions during the summer that require four to six hours. Riding the rails is great fun! My favorite section of track is alongside the Tuckaseegee River between Dillsboro and Bryson City.

Nantahala National Forest

The Nantahala National Forest contains over one million acres of forest and offers many developed forest service campgrounds that you might want to try instead of fighting the masses in the Park. These campgrounds are inexpensive and not usually crowded, except on weekends in mid-summer or October.

You can generally camp anywhere in the national forest that is not specifically posted. The USDA publication, *National Forests in North Carolina*, which is available at ranger stations, lists national forest attractions, recreational areas, and points of interest, as well as dozens of national forest campgrounds.

You may want to check out the Snowbird Mountains, which offer 40 miles of backcountry trails, along with mountain streams and waterfalls. *The Snowbird Area Trail Map*, available for sale at ranger stations and camping stores, provides information about the trails and camping regulations.

Shining Rock Wilderness Area and Middle Fork Wilderness Area, located along the Blue Ridge Parkway near Waynesville, offer extensive hiking and backpacking trips. Dozens of trails criss-cross grassy balds along the high ridge near the impressive white quartz vein that gives the area its name, Shining Rock. Other trails lead through lower elevations where there are spectacular displays of spring wildflowers. Because of heavy use, open fires are no longer allowed in Shining Rock Wilderness, so be sure to bring a backpacking stove. For maps and more information, contact the District Ranger in Pisgah Forest (see Appendix C).

Joyce Kilmer and Slickrock-Citico Wilderness Areas

Joyce Kilmer is a small park contained in one valley with a loop trail around the perimeter and a main trail through the middle following a stream to its headwaters. This area is known for its large trees and lush undergrowth of rhododendron, mosses, and ferns.

Two watershed divides, the Slickrock and the Citico, adjoin Kilmer and provide an additional 60 miles of hiking trails. The lower ends of these streams were heavily logged years ago, but the forests have regrown beautifully, and there are exceptional stands of old growth trees at the headwaters of both drainages. Camping is only allowed in the Slickrock Wilderness Area.

For additional information, contact the Nantahala National Forest in North Carolina and the Cherokee National Forest in southeastern Tennessee (see Appendix C). The for-sale publication *Joyce Kilmer-Slickrock Wilderness and Citico Creek Wilderness* provides additional information and a map of the trails.

Appendix A

Summary of Recommended Trails

The following table is a summary of the 140 trails described in this book. In general, the higher the average elevation change, shown as feet per mile, the more difficult the trail and slower the hike times.

Difficulty of the hike can be estimated using the following as a guide:

Easy—less than 150 ft. elevation change per mile
Moderate—between 150-400 ft. elevation change per mile
Strenuous—between 400-700 ft. elevation change per mile
Extremely Strenuous—greater than 700 ft. elevation change per mile

Trail # and Name	Mileage	Elevation Change	Average (feet/mile)
1 Appalachian Trail	70	*	138

Hiked south to north, the Appalachian Trail has an elevation change of +9700/-9600. Preferred travel is south to north

Cattaloochee Area

Trail # and Name	Mileage	Elevation Change	Average (feet/mile)
2 Boogerman Trail	3.8	900 feet	237
3 Caldwell Fork Trail	4.8	1360	283
4 Rough Fork Trail	6.5	2380	366
5 Polls Gap/ Spruce Mtn.	5.5	840	153
6 Cataloochee Divide Trail	6.4	1470	230
7 Hemphill Bald Trail	8.5	1800	212
8 McKee Branch Trail	2.3	1710	743
9 Big Fork Ridge Trail	3.1	820	265
10 Little Cataloochee Trail	5.2	900	173
11 Long Bunk Trail	3.7	900	443
12 Mt. Sterling Gap Trail	2.3	1945	846
13 Mt. Sterling Ridge Trail	6.0	900	150
14 Pretty Hollow Gap Trail	5.2	2190	421
15 Balsam Mountain Trail	10.8	1640	152
16 Palmer Creek Trail	3.3	1770	536
17 Flat Creek Trail	2.6	440	169

Trail # and Name	Mileage	Elevation Change	Average (feet/mile)
Cosby-Big Creek Area			
18 Gabes Mountain Trail	6.6	1300	197
19 Maddron Bald Trail	7.2	2600	361
20 Snake Den Ridge Trail	4.6	3400	739
21 Lower Mt. Cammerer Tr.	7.4	1300	176
22 Cosby Creek/Low Gap Tr.	2.5	1800	720
23 Mt. Cammerer Side Trail	0.6	70	117
24 Baxter Creek Trail	6.2	4150	669
25 Big Creek Trail	5.0	1380	276
26 Chestnut Branch Trail	2.0	1100	550
27 Low Gap Trail	2.3	1240	539
28 Swallow Fork Trail	4.0	2180	545
29 Gunter Fork Trail	4.0	2400	600
30 Camel Gap Trail	4.1	1610	322
Mt. LeConte-Greenbrier Area			
31 Alum Cave Bluff Trail	4.9	2560	522
32 Boulevard Trail	5.3	1080	204
33 Trillium Gap Trail	6.5	3300	507
34 Rainbow Falls Trail	6.0	3820	637
35 Bullhead Trail	5.9	3820	647
36 Brushy Mountain Trail	4.8	3010	627
37 Ramsey Cascade Trail	4.0	1600	400
38 Porters Creek Trail	2.7	1600	593
39 Old Settlers Trail	15.9	1300	82
40 Twin Creeks Trail	1.8	800	444
41 Grapeyard Ridge Trail	7.6	700	92
42 Baskins Creek Trail	2.7	700	259
43 Prong Trail	2.6	1000	385
44 W. Prong Little River Tr.	3.1	1000	326
Elkmont-Tremont Area			
45 Chimney Tops Trail	1.1	1350	1227
46 Road Prong Trail	2.4	1870	779
47 Little River Trail	4.7	1400	298

Trail # and Name	Mileage	Elevation Change	Average (feet/mile)
48 Cucumber Gap Trail	2.3	320	139
49 Huskey Gap Trail	4.1	1200	600
50 Sugarland Mt. Trail	12.1	3700	306
51 Rough Creek Trail	2.8	1530	546
52 Goshen Prong Trail	7.3	3020	414
53 Laurel Falls Trail	4.0	1780	445
54 Cove Mt. Trail	8.6	2580	300
55 Little Greenbrier Ridge Tr.	4.3	1780	414
56 Little Brier Gap Trail	2.0	500	250
57 Roundtop Trail	7.6	1500	197
58 Chestnut Top Trail	4.3	960	223
59 Scott Mountain Trail	3.6	1600	444
60 Meigs Mt. Trail	6.0	1150	192
61 Lumber Ridge Trail	4.0	1450	362
62 Curry Mountain Trail	3.3	1100	333
63 Meigs Creek Trail	3.3	840	255
64 Jakes Creek (to Blanket Mt)	3.7	2260	611
65 Miry Ridge Trail	4.9	900	184
66 Panther Creek Trail	2.3	1460	635
67 Middle Prong Trail	4.1	1575	384
68 Greenbrier Ridge Trail	4.2	1280	305
69 West Prong Trail	2.7	650	241
70 Finley Cane Trail	2.7	650	241
71 Bote Mountain Trail	9.1	3290	361
72 Turkeypen Ridge Trail	3.6	250	69

Cades Cove-Abrams Creek-Rich Mountain Area

73 Anthony Creek Trail	3.2	1860	581
74 Russell Field Trail	3.5	1860	531
75 Rich Mt. Loop Trail	7.5	1740	232
76 Rich Mountain Trail	4.0	1480	370
77 Cooper Road Trail	10.5	800	143
78 Beard Cane Trail	4.2	400	95
79 Ace Gap Trail	5.6	440	79
80 Cane Gap Trail	2.8	500	178
81 Cane Creek Trail	2.1	400	190

Trail # and Name	Mileage	Elevation Change	Average (feet/mile)
82 Goldmine Trail	0.8	400	500
83 Abrams Falls Trail	4.2	800	190
84 Hatcher Mountain Trail	2.8	600	214
85 Scott Gap-Abrams Creek	1.8	500	278
86 Little Bottoms Trail	2.3	400	174
87 Rabbit Creek Trail	7.6	1240	163
88 Hannah Mt. Trail	7.6	1160	153
89 Gregory Bald Trail	7.1	2170	306
90 Gregory Ridge Trail	4.9	2600	473

Twentymile Creek-Eagle Creek Area

Trail # and Name	Mileage	Elevation Change	Average (feet/mile)
91 Twentymile Creek Trail	4.5	2355	523
92 Twentymile Loop Trail	2.8	500	333
93 Long Hungry Ridge Trail	4.5	2240	498
94 Wolf Ridge Trail	6.5	2650	408
95 Western Lakeshore Trail	5.5	400	73
96 Eagle Creek Trail	9.0	3170	352
97 Lost Cove Trail	3.5	1930	551
98 Pinnacle Creek Trail	3.5	1164	333

Middle Creeks—Hazel, Forney, Noland Creeks

Trail # and Name	Mileage	Elevation Change	Average (feet/mile)
99 Lakeshore Trail	25.0	1900	76
100 Hazel Creek Trail	11.8	3580	256
101 Sugar Fork Trail	2.5	775	337
102 Jenkins Ridge Trail	6.0	2076	346
103 Bone Valley Trail	1.5	100	67
104 Cold Spring Gap Trail	4.0	2450	612
105 Welch Ridge Trail	6.5	2100	323
106 Forney Creek Trail	10.0	4030	403
107 Forney Ridge Trail	5.0	2500	500
108 Bear Creek Trail	5.8	3100	534
109 Jonas Creek Trail	4.5	2200	489
110 Noland Creek Trail	10.5	2500	238
111 Tunnel Trail	0.7	100	100
112 Goldmine Loop Trail	4.0	900	225
113 White Oak Branch Trail	2.0	400	200

Trail # and Name	Mileage	Elevation Change	Average (feet/mile)
114 Noland Divide Trail	11.8	4150	352
115/116 Springhouse Branch Trail	8.3	1400	430

Deep Creek Area

117 Deep Creek Trail	13.7	2820	206
118 Pole Road Creek Trail	3.3	1800	545
119 Fork Ridge Trail	5.2	2880	554
120 Thomas Divide Trail	13.7	2600	190
121 Sunkota Ridge Trail	8.7	2780	320
122 Deeplow Gap Trail	8.7	2560	294
123 Indian Creek Road Trail	4.4	1530	348
124 Indian Creek Rd. Trail	2.0	1000	500

Bradley Fork-Oconaluftee-Raven Fork Area

125 Newton Bald Trail	6.0	2900	483
126 Kanati Fork Trail	3.0	2110	703
127 Bradley Fork Trail	5.3	920	174
128 Smokemont Loop Trail	5.5	1240	225
129 Dry Sluice Gap Trail	3.8	2540	668
130 Kephart Prong Trail	2.0	830	415
131 Grassy Branch Trail	2.5	1740	696
132 Sweat Heifer Creek Trail	3.7	2270	614
133 Lower Hughes Ridge Tr.	7.3	2760	378
134 Upper Hughes Ridge Tr.	4.7	1000	213
135 Hyatt Ridge Trail	4.2	2065	490
136 Taywa Creek Trail	3.3	2130	645
137 Chasteen Creek Trail	4.1	2300	561
138 Enloe Creek Trail	3.6	1200	444
139 Hyatt Bald Trail	2.8	1880	671
140 Beech Gap Trail	4.5	2900	644

Auto Touring. The Great Smoky Mountain Natural History Association, 1989.

A large number of publications concerning the Smokies are
available through the GSMNHA bookstores at the main visitor
centers. They produce a nice set of informational leaflets (about
$.25 each) and maps: *Auto Touring, Forests and Wildflowers, Streams
& Waterfalls, Mountain People, Walks & Hikes,* and *Wildlife.* These
contain mileage charts and recommended trails with distances
and difficulty.

*The Best of the Great Smoky Mountains National Park: A Hiker's Guide to
Trails and Attractions,* by Russ Manning and Sondra Jamieson. Norris,
TN: Mountain Laural Place, 1991 (246 pages).

Recently published, this book details sixty-five trails in the Park
and offers mile-by-mile details of the trails. This is a good
substitute for the out-of-print book by Murlless and Stallings.

*Bicycling The Blue Ridge: A Guide to the Skyline Drive and the Blue Ridge
Parkway,* by Elizabeth and Charlie Skinner. Birmingham, AL: Menasha
Ridge Press, 1990 (173 pages).

This book is not just for biking. It offers details on how to best
enjoy the Skyline Drive and the Blue Ridge Parkway at a bicyclist's
pace and point of view. The elevation maps and summaries are
excellent!

Birth of a National Park in the Great Smoky Mountains, by Carlos
Campbell. Knoxville, TN: University of Tennessee Press, 1960 (154
pages).

This is an excellent history on politics, land acquisitions, and
personality struggles involving the formation of the Park.

Connecting People and Nature: A Collection of the Lesson Plans Used at Great Smoky Mountains Institute at Tremont. Great Smoky Mountains Institute at Tremont, 1989. (new addition, 1994)

This is a wonderful collection of lesson plans developed by the staff of Great Smoky Mountains Institute at Tremont for students of all ages. It has been time tested over a period of five years and includes a dozen three-hour lessons for small groups and larger groups, as well as all-day programs, background information, and teacher activities. This collection is absolutely recommended for anyone interested in earth education, specifically about the Southern Appalachians.

Geology of the Great Smoky Mountains National Park, Tennessee and North Carolina, by Philip King, R.B. Neuman, and J.B. Hadley. USDA Geological Survey Professional Paper 587, 1968 (23 pages).

A concise guide to the geology of the area, this book includes a full-color map of rock types, formations, and fault zones. It is great for understanding the forces that have created and carved the mountains and for discovering waterfalls and finding faults.

The Great Smokies: A Wonderment of Mountains, Selected Columns by Carson Brewer. Knoxville, TN: Tenpenny Publishing, 1981 (198 pages).

Carson Brewer wrote for the *Knoxville News-Sentinel* for 35 years. This book is a collection of his best and most humorous columns. They provide informative, personal insights into life in the Smokies.

Great Smoky Mountains Wildflowers, by Carlos Campbell, W.F. Hutson, and A. J. Sharp. Knoxville, TN: University of Tennessee Press, 4th edition, 1977 (113 pages).

This is a color-photo guide to flowers of the Smokies. While not nearly as botanical as Stupka, it makes a nice, inexpensive set of wildflowers photos.

Hiking Trails of the Smokies, Great Smoky Mountains Natural History Association, 1994. (574 pages).

This brand new trail book is an excellent update to the out-of-print Sierra Club's Hiker's Guide to the Smokies. Fifteen authors provide detailed trail information, water sources, and natural history. Each trail has a profile map which helps hikers to visualize trail difficulty. This book is a must for any extensive trip into the backcountry of the Smokies.

Hiking in the Great Smokies, by Carson Brewer. Knoxville, TN: S. B. Newman Printing, 1962 (66 pages).

This is a guide to short day hikes (over two dozen) in the Park. I found it well-written and accurate, although minor trail changes have occurred. This inexpensive "book" is great if you plan on car-camping and day hiking.

Hiking Map and Guide: Great Smoky Mountains National Park, by Helen H. Larson. Earthwalk Press, 1990.

This beautifully made, large-scale topographical map of the Smokies includes nearby hiking and horse trails. This map also includes brief information about the Park, backcountry regulations, safety considerations, and a table of trail mileage and brief descriptions.

Mountain Roads and Quiet Places: A Complete Guide to the Roads of Great Smoky Mountains National Park, by Jerry DeLaughter. Great Smoky Mountains Natural History Association, 1986 (96 pages).

This book is a wonderful guide to 13 recommended road tours in and around the Park. It is a great introduction to the roads and some recommended trails in the Park. A nice souvenir!

Off the Beaten Track: A Guide to Mountain Biking in Western North Carolina, by Jim Parham. Almond, NC: WMC Publishing, 1992 (70 pages).

This guide details 25 mountain bike trails in western North Carolina, mostly within an hour drive from the western end of the Smokies. Great resource!

A Roadside Guide to the Geology of the Great Smoky Mountains National Park, by Harry L. Moore. Knoxville, TN: University of Tennessee Press, 1988 (178 pages).

Organized as a mile-by-mile guide to roadside geological features, this excellent photographic guide covers five major road sections and five important trails. It includes information on the geological strata and events that have shaped the mountains.

Scenic Drives and Wildflower Walks in the Great Smokies. Knoxville Garden Club, 1990 (93 pages).
This is a guide to recommended auto routes and day hikes where you can find the wildflowers of the Smokies. It includes a unique monthly timetable to the best areas.

Strangers in High Places: The Story of the Great Smoky Mountains, by Michael Frome. Knoxville, TN: University of Tennessee Press, 2nd edition, 1980 (391 pages).
This book describes the settlement and development of the Park and is one of my favorite on the history and people of the region.

Time Well Spent: Family Hiking in the Smokies, by Hal Hubbs, Charles Maynard, and David Morris. Seymour, TN: Panther Press, 1991 (69 pages).
This book details 25 trails and has an excellent index with trail mileage, estimated hiking times, and trail descriptions. It is family-oriented and includes references to nature, historical, and auto trails. It is less detailed than Manning and Jamieson, but it is good for the lite-hiker!

Smoky Mountain Trail Guide, by Fogel Clark. Southern Pines, NC: Recreational Publications, 1979.
This is basically a map of the area with information on specific areas on the back. This is one of my favorite maps because it has topographical details and allows you to compare large areas at a glance. The trail details are very accurate and I highly recommend it for beginner and advanced hikers alike.

Smoky Mountain Trout Fishing Guide, by Don Kirk. Birmingham, AL: Menasha Ridge Press, 1993 (160 pages).
This delightful guide to the trout waters of the Park contains detailed information on over 140 streams and includes references to USGS Quadrangle maps. It is an incredible resource that cites stream size, fishing pressure, quality, and access.

The Great Smoky Mountains, by Laura Thornborough. Knoxville, TN: University of Tennessee Press, 1937 (224 pages).

The author was in love with the Smokies and spent much time describing the area and the development of the Park. She especially loved the people and settlers around Gatlinburg. She published before extensive trail systems were developed in the Park.

A Traveler's Guide to the Smoky Mountains Region, by Jeff Bradley. Mississippi: Harvard Common Press, 1985 (270 pages).

This excellent, extremely well-written, and humorous guide to the mountainous areas adjacent to the Park stresses nearby towns, attractions, recommended museums, dining, and events. Did you know they hung an elephant for murder in Erwin, Tennessee? Delightfully humorous!

Trees, Shrubs and Woody Vines of the Great Smoky Mountains National Park, by Arthur Stupka. Knoxville, TN: University of Tennessee Press, 1964 (86 pages).

This book is a botanical index/key to the flora of the Smokies. Stupka was a long-term naturalist in the Park and really knows his stuff! This is a good source for additional botanical references.

Walking Softly in the Wilderness: The Sierra Club Guide to Backpacking, by John Hart. Sierra Club Books, 2nd edition, 1984 (500 pages).

This is a great, inclusive guide to fundamentals of low-impact backpacking and camping. It is highly recommended for its equipment review and environmentally-sound philosophy.

Waterfalls and Cascades of the Great Smoky Mountains, by Hal Hubbs, Charles Maynard, and David Morris. Seymour, TN: Panther Press, 1992 (79 pages).

This guide to 29 waterfalls in the Smokies is the best guide to the falls in the Park. It has excellent photographs of 20 falls (most in color!).

Important Addresses

Almond Boat and RV Park (Fontana Lake), (704) 488-6423.

Appalachian Trail Conference, 799 Washington St., Harpers Ferry, WV 25425, (304) 535-6331.

Backcountry Reservations, Great Smoky Mountains National Park, Gatlinburg, TN 37738, (423) 436-1231 (M-F 8:00 A.M. to 6:00 P.M.).

Benton McKaye Trail Association, P.O. Box 53271, Atlanta, GA 30355-1271.

Cades Cove Horse Concession, (423) 448-6286.

Campground Reservations (only for Cades Cove, Elkmont, and Smokemont—reservations required May 15th to October 30), (800) 365-CAMP (Park code is GREA, or wait for operator). Mail reservations to: Destinet Reservations, 9450 Carroll Park Dr., SanDiego, CA 92121.

Carolina Mountain Hiking Club, P.O. Box 68, Asheville, NC 28802.

Carolina Outfitters Rafting, 12121 Hwy. 19, Bryson City, NC 28713. (800) GOT-RAFT or (704) 488-6345.

Chattahoochee National Forest (Georgia), 1755 Cleveland Hwy., Gainesville, GA 30501, (770) 536-0641.

Cheoah Ranger District (Robbinsville), (704) 479-6431.

Cherokee National Forest (Tennessee), P.O. Box 2010, Cleveland, TN 37320, (615) 476-9700.

Cherokee River Trips, 172 Highway 19 South, Cherokee, NC 28719, (704) 497-2821.

Cherokee Tribal Travel and Promotion, P.O. Box 460, Cherokee, NC 28719 (located at junction of US 19/441), (704) 497-9195, (800) 222-6157 (in NC), or (800) 438-1601 (outside NC).

Deep Creek Horse Concession, (704) 497-8504.

Fast River Rafts, 14690 Highway 19 West, Bryson City, NC 28713, (800) 438-7238 or (704) 488-2386.

Fontana Marina, (704) 498-2211.

Fontana Village Resort, P.O. Box 68, Hwy 28, Fontana Dam, NC 28733, (800) 849-2258 or (704) 498-2211.

French Broad Ranger District (Hot Springs), (704) 622-3202.

Gatlinburg Chamber, P.O. Box 527, Gatlinburg, TN 37738, (423) 453-5700, (800) 824-4766 (in TN), or (800) 568-4748 (outside TN).

Grandfather Ranger District (Nebo), (704) 652-2144.

Great Smoky Mountains National Park Superintendent, Gatlinburg, TN 37738, (423) 436-1200.

Great Smoky Mountains Natural History Association, 115 Park Headquarters Road, Gatlinburg 37738, (615) 436-7318.

Great Smoky Mountain Railroad, 119 Front Street, Dillsboro, NC 28725, (800) 872-4681 or (704) 586-8811 (in NC).

Greater Haywood County Chamber of Commerce, 1133 N. Main St., Suite 1-40, Waynesville, NC 28786, (704) 452-0152 or (800) 334-9036 (outside NC).

Highlands Ranger District (Highlands), (704) 526-3765.

Jackson County Chamber of Commerce, 18 North Central Street, Sylva, NC 28779, (704) 586-2155.

LeConte Lodge, P.O. Box 350, Gatlinburg, TN 37738, (423) 429-5704.

Maggie Valley Chamber of Commerce, P.O. Box 87, Maggie Valley, NC 28751 (located on south US 19), (704) 926-1686 or (800) 785-8259 (outside NC).

McCarter Horse Concession (near Sugarlands), (423) 436-5354.

Nantahala Outdoor Center, 13077 Highway 19 West, Bryson City, NC 28713, (800) 232-7238 or (704) 488-2175.

Nantahala Rafts, 14260 Hwy. 19 West, Bryson City, NC 28713, (800) 245-7700 or (704) 488-2325.

Nantahala-Pisgah National Forest, P.O. Box 2750, Asheville, NC 28802, (704) 298-0398.

North Carolina Bartram Trail Society c/o Mo Wheeler, Secretary, P.O. Box 428D, Highlands, NC 28741.

North Carolina Department of Natural Resources and Community Development, Division of Parks and Recreation, P.O. Box 27687, Raleigh, NC 27611, (919) 733-4181 (source of NC Camping and Outdoors Directory).

North Carolina Department of Transportation, Bicycle Coordinator, P.O. Box 25201, Raleigh, NC 27611, (919) 733-2804.

North Carolina Division of Travel and Tourism, 301 N. Wilmington St., Raleigh, NC 27626, (800) VISIT NC or (919) 733-4171 (in NC).

North Carolina Road Conditions, (800) 662-7956.

North Carolina State Highway Patrol (Peachtree), (704) 837-6804.

North Carolina State Highway Patrol (Bryson City), (704) 479-3352.

North Carolina State Highway Patrol (Hayesville-Murphy), (704) 837-6804.

North Carolina Weather Conditions (Oconaluftee Visitor Center), (704) 497-1900.

North Carolina Wildlife Resources Commission, (800) 662-7137 (to report hunting violations, etc.).

Paddle Inn Rafting Company, 48 Highway 19 West, Bryson City, NC 28713, (704) 488-9651.

Pigeon Forge Department of Tourism, Pigeon Forge, TN 37863, (615) 453-8574.

Pigeon River Outdoors, P.O. Box 592, Gatlinburg, NC 37738, (800) 776-7238 or (423) 436-5008.

Pisgah Ranger District (Pisgah Forest), (704) 877-3265.

Rolling Thunder River Company, P.O. Box 88, Almond, NC 28702, (800) 408-RAFT or (704) 488-2030.

Sevierville Chamber of Commerce, 866 Winfield Dunn Pkwy., Sevierville, TN 37876, (615) 453-6411.

Smokemont Horse Concession, (704) 497-2373.

Smoky Mountain Hiking Club, P.O. Box 1454, Knoxville, TN 37901.

Smoky Mountain Host of North Carolina, 4437 Georgia Rd., Franklin, NC 28734, (800) 432-HOST or (704) 369-9606.

Smoky Mountain Riding Stables, (704) 436-5634.

Swain County Chamber of Commerce Center, P.O. Box 509, Bryson City, NC 28713, (704) 488-3681.

Tennessee Tourism, 320 6th Avenue North #500, Nashville, TN 37203.

Tennessee Weather Conditions (Sugarlands Visitor Center/Park Headquarters), (615) 436-1200.

Toecane Ranger District (Burnsville), (704) 682-6146.

Tuckaseegee Outfitters, P.O. Box 1719, Cullowhee, NC 28723, (704) 586-5050 (whitewater float trips on the Tuckaseegee River).

Tusquitee Ranger District (Murphy), (704) 837-5152.

USA Raft, 11044 Hwy. 19 West, Bryson City, NC 28713, (800) USA-RAFT or (704) 488-3316.

Wayah Ranger District (Franklin), (704) 524-6441.

Wildwater, Ltd., Nantahala Rafting Center, P.O. Drawer 430, Bryson City, NC 28713, (800) 451-9972 or (704) 488-2384.

Colophon

The text of this book was set in a digital version of Palatino, a typeface created by noted type designer Hermann Zapf in 1950 for the Stempel Foundry. The design is Zapf's modern interpretation of 16th-century calligraphy. The display type was set in Helvetica Light Extended. The text was designed by Frank Logue and composed by Carolina Graphics Group in Rome, Georgia. The cover design is by Leslie Cummins.

Hwy 28 to 74
74 W
right side
2'6 miles pass intersection
$91.80

Andy
Nantahala River *2!*3
GG0270
July 6 10⁰⁰